PENGUIN BOOKS

NOT NOW, NOT EVER

Julia Gillard was the 27th Prime Minister of Australia, the first, and only, woman to serve in that role. Since leaving office, she has dedicated her time to advocacy, governance roles and writing. In 2021, Julia was appointed Chair of Wellcome, a global charitable foundation based in the United Kingdom that supports science to solve urgent worldwide health challenges. Julia is also the founder and inaugural Chair of the Global Institute for Women's Leadership at King's College London and Chair of its sister institute at the Australian National University. GIWL strives for a world where being a woman is neither a barrier to becoming a leader in any field, nor a contributor to negative perceptions of an individual's leadership. In 2014, Julia joined the Board of Beyond Blue, one of Australia's foremost mental health awareness bodies, and has served as Chair since 2017. As a lifelong advocate for increasing access to education, especially in developing nations, Julia was Chair of the Global Partnership for Education from 2014 to 2021. Julia wrote *My Story*, a memoir based on her experience as prime minister. Her second book, *Women and Leadership: Real lives, real lessons*, co-authored with Dr Ngozi Okonjo-Iweala, explores the challenges women face in leadership. *Not Now, Not Ever* is her third book.

Also by Julia Gillard

My Story

Women and Leadership: Real lives, real lessons
(with Ngozi Okonjo-Iweala)

Ten years on from
the misogyny speech

NOT NOW, NOT EVER

EDITED BY JULIA GILLARD

PENGUIN BOOKS

PENGUIN BOOKS

UK | USA | Canada | Ireland | Australia
India | New Zealand | South Africa | China

Penguin Books is part of the Penguin Random House group of companies
whose addresses can be found at global.penguinrandomhouse.com

First published by Vintage in 2022
This edition published by Penguin Books in 2024

Cover design and illustration by Christa Moffitt, Christabella
Designs © Penguin Random House Australia Pty Ltd
Author photograph by Nick Clayton
Typeset in Minion Pro by Midland Typesetters, Australia

Printed and bound in Australia by Griffin Press, an accredited
ISO AS/NZS 14001 Environmental Management Systems printer

A catalogue record for this
book is available from the
National Library of Australia

ISBN 978 1 76134 344 5

penguin.com.au

We at Penguin Random House Australia acknowledge that Aboriginal and Torres Strait
Islander peoples are the Traditional Custodians and the first storytellers of the lands on
which we live and work. We honour Aboriginal and Torres Strait Islander peoples'
continuous connection to Country, waters, skies and communities. We celebrate
Aboriginal and Torres Strait Islander stories, traditions and living cultures;
and we pay our respects to Elders past and present.

For every woman who has thought to herself,
'That's not fair, that's not right, it wouldn't happen to a man.'
Let's turn those thoughts into deeds, those deeds into
a powerful wave of change, and that frustration
into a gender equal future.

Contents

Part Three Fighting misogyny

Prologue

The misogyny speech

I rise to oppose the motion moved by the Leader of the Opposition, and in so doing I say to the Leader of the Opposition: I will not be lectured about sexism and misogyny by this man. I will not. The government will not be lectured about sexism and misogyny by this man. Not now, not ever. The Leader of the Opposition says that people who hold sexist views and who are misogynists are not appropriate for high office. Well, I hope the Leader of the Opposition has a piece of paper and he is writing out his resignation, because if he wants to know what misogyny looks like in modern Australia he does not need a motion in the House of Representatives; he needs a mirror. That is what he needs.

Let's go through the opposition leader's repulsive double standards when it comes to misogyny and sexism. We are now supposed to take seriously that the Leader of the Opposition is offended by Mr Slipper's text messages, when this is what the Leader of the Opposition said when he was a minister under the last government – not when he was a student, not when he was in high school but when he was a minister under the last government. In a discussion about women being under-represented in institutions of power in Australia, the interviewer was a man called Stavros and the Leader of the Opposition said: 'If it's true, Stavros, that men have more power, generally speaking, than women, is that a bad thing?'

Then a discussion ensued and another person being interviewed said, 'I want my daughter to have as much opportunity as my son,' to which the Leader of the Opposition said: 'Yes, I completely agree, but what if men are by physiology or temperament more adapted to exercise authority or to issue command?' Then ensues another discussion about women's role in modern society, and the other person participating in the discussions says, 'I think it's very hard to deny that there is an under-representation of women,' to which the Leader of the Opposition says, 'But there's an assumption that this is a bad thing.' This is the man from whom we are supposed to take lectures about sexism!

And it goes on. I was very offended personally when the Leader of the Opposition as minister for health said, 'Abortion is the easy way out.' I was very personally offended by those comments. He said that in March 2004, and I suggest he check the records. I was also very offended on behalf of the women of Australia when in the course of the carbon pricing campaign the Leader of the Opposition said, 'What the housewives of Australia need to understand as they do the ironing.' Thank you for that painting of women's roles in modern Australia! Then, of course, I am offended by the sexism, by the misogyny, of the Leader of the Opposition catcalling across this table at me as I sit here as Prime Minister, 'if the Prime Minister wants to, politically speaking, make an honest woman of herself' – something that would never have been said to any man sitting in this chair.

I was offended when the Leader of the Opposition went outside the front of the parliament and stood next to a sign that said 'Ditch the witch'. I was offended when the Leader of the Opposition stood next to a sign that described me as a man's bitch. I was offended by those things. It is misogyny, sexism, every day from this Leader of the Opposition. Every day, in every way, across the time the Leader of the Opposition has sat in that chair and I have sat in this chair, that is all we have heard from him.

Now the Leader of the Opposition wants to be taken seriously. Apparently he has woken up, after this track record and all of these statements, and has gone, 'Oh dear, there is this thing called sexism; oh my lord, there is this thing called misogyny. Who is one of them? The Speaker must be because that suits my political purpose.' He does not turn a hair about any of his past statements; does not walk into this parliament and apologise to the women of Australia; does not walk into this parliament and apologise to me for the things that have come out of his mouth – but he now seeks to use this as a battering ram against someone else. This kind of hypocrisy should not be tolerated, which is why this motion from the Leader of the Opposition should not be taken seriously.

Second, the Leader of the Opposition is always wonderful at walking into this parliament and giving me and others a lecture about what they should take responsibility for. He is always wonderful about everything that I should take responsibility for, now apparently including the text messages of the member for Fisher. He is always keen to say others should assume responsibility, particularly me. Can anybody remind me whether the Leader of the Opposition has taken any responsibility for the conduct of the Sydney Young Liberals and the attendance at their event of members of his frontbench? Has he taken any responsibility for the conduct of members of his political party and members of his frontbench, who apparently when the most vile things were being said about my family raised no voice of objection.

No one walked out of the room, no one walked up to Mr Jones and said that this was not acceptable. Instead, it was all viewed as good fun – until it was run in a Sunday newspaper, and then the Leader of the Opposition and others started ducking for cover. He is big on lectures on responsibility; very light on accepting responsibility himself for the vile conduct of members of his political party.

I turn to the third reason why the Leader of the Opposition should not be taken seriously on this motion. The Leader of the Opposition and the Deputy Leader of the Opposition have come into this place and talked about the member for Fisher. Let me remind the opposition, and the Leader of the Opposition particularly, about their track record and association with the member for Fisher. I remind them that the National Party preselected the member for Fisher for the 1984 election, that the National Party preselected the member for Fisher for the 1987 election, and that the Liberal Party preselected the member for Fisher for the 1993 election, then for the 1996 election, then for the 1998 election, then for the 2001 election, then for the 2004 election, then for the 2007 election and then for the 2010 election. Across many of those preselections Mr Slipper enjoyed the personal support of the Leader of the Opposition. I remind the Leader of the Opposition that on 28 September 2010, following the last election campaign when Mr Slipper was elected as Deputy Speaker, the Leader of the Opposition referred to the member for Maranoa, who was also elected to a position at the same time, and went on:

. . . the member for Maranoa and the member for Fisher will serve as a fine complement to the member for Scullin in the chair. I believe that the parliament will be well served by the team which will occupy the chair in this chamber . . . I congratulate the member for Fisher, who has been a friend of mine for a very long time who has served this parliament in many capacities with distinction . . .

They are the words of the Leader of the Opposition on record about his personal friendship with Mr Slipper and on record about his view of Mr Slipper's qualities and attributes to be the Speaker. There is no walking away from those words – they were the statements of the Leader of the Opposition then.

I remind the Leader of the Opposition, who now comes in here and speaks about Mr Slipper and apparently his inability to work with or talk to Mr Slipper, that he attended Mr Slipper's wedding. Did he walk up to Mr Slipper in the middle of the service and say he was disgusted to be there? Was that the attitude he took? No, he attended that wedding as a friend. The Leader of the Opposition is keen to lecture others about what they ought to know or did know about Mr Slipper but, with respect, I would say to the Leader of the Opposition that, after a long personal association, including attending Mr Slipper's wedding, it would be interesting to know whether the Leader of the Opposition was surprised by these text messages. He is certainly in a position to speak more intimately about Mr Slipper than I am and many other people in this parliament are, given this long personal association. Then, of course, the Leader of the Opposition comes into this place and says:

And every day the Prime Minister stands in this parliament to defend this Speaker will be another day of shame for this parliament; another day of shame for a government which should already have died of shame.

I indicate to the Leader of the Opposition that the government is not dying of shame – and my father did not die of shame. What the Leader of the Opposition should be ashamed of is his performance in this parliament and the sexism he brings with it.

[Government and opposition members interjecting]

That is a direct quote from the Leader of the Opposition, so I suggest those groaning have a word with him.

On the conduct of Mr Slipper and on the text messages which are in the public domain – I have seen the press reports of those text messages and I am offended by their content. I am offended by their content because I am always offended by sexism. I am offended by their content because I am always offended by statements which are anti-women. I am offended by those things in the same way I have been offended by things the Leader of the Opposition has said and no doubt will continue to say in the future – because if this, today, was an exhibition of his new feminine side, I do not think we have much to look forward to in terms of changed conduct.

I am offended by those text messages but I also believe that, in making a decision about the speakership, this parliament should recognise that there is a court case in progress and that the judge has reserved his decision. Having waited for a number of months for the legal matters surrounding Mr Slipper to come to a conclusion, this parliament should see that conclusion. I believe that is the appropriate path forward and that people will then have an opportunity to make up their minds with the fullest information available to them.

But, whenever people make up their minds about those questions, what I will not stand for – what I will never stand for – is the Leader of the Opposition coming into this place and peddling a double standard. I will not stand for him peddling a standard for Mr Slipper he would not set for himself, peddling a standard for Mr Slipper he has not set for other members of his frontbench or peddling a standard for Mr Slipper which has not been met by the people – such as his former shadow parliamentary secretary, Senator Bernardi – who have been sent out to say the vilest and most revolting things. I will not ever allow the Leader of the Opposition to impose his double standards on this parliament.

Sexism should always be unacceptable. We should always conduct ourselves in such a way as to make it clear that it is unacceptable. The Leader of the Opposition says, 'Do something.' He could do something himself if he wanted to deal with sexism in this parliament. He could change his behaviour, he could apologise for all his past statements and he could apologise for standing next to signs describing me as a witch and a bitch – terminology now objected to by the frontbench of the opposition. He could change standards himself if he sought to do so. But we will see none of that from the Leader of the Opposition, because on these questions he is incapable of change. He is capable of double standards but incapable of change. His double standards should not rule this parliament.

Good sense, common sense and proper process are what should rule this parliament. That is what I believe is the path forward for this parliament, not the kinds of double standards and political game playing imposed by the Leader of the Opposition, who is now looking at his watch because, apparently, a woman has spoken for too long – I have, in the past, had him yell at me to shut up.

But I will take the remaining seconds of my speaking time to say to the Leader of the Opposition that I think the best course for him is to reflect on the standards he has exhibited in public life, on the responsibility he should take for his public statements, on his close personal connection with Peter Slipper and on the hypocrisy he has displayed in this House today. On that basis, because of the Leader of the Opposition's motivations, this parliament should today reject this motion, and the Leader of the Opposition should think seriously about the role of women in public life and in Australian society – because we are entitled to a better standard than this.

On Tuesday 9 October I was at Admiralty House, the Sydney residence of the governor-general. A busy day: an investiture ceremony in the morning and a formal dinner in the evening for Care Australia. Michael usually watched Question Time. He called me just as the prime minister spoke. I listened intently, stunned. Absolutely stunned. Then furious and then a deep feeling of relief as Ms Gillard confronted the disgraceful, debilitating insults, the personal denigrations, slimy innuendos, hideous slogans and images – with powerful, searing emotion, speaking out loud and clear.

As I write these words I feel my heart thumping as it did on that afternoon ten years ago.

I thought then as I do now of that glorious late winter morning in Canberra when I swore our first woman prime minister into office; the rapturous applause, the joyous celebration across our nation, the message it carried to our young ones, especially our girls.

I thought of the courage. The pain that drove the speech that has gripped the world since.

And the regret that *we* as one had not called out – Stop. No More. Never again – when the misogynistic course of conduct began.

We must never forget that the most important tool we have is our voice. Not now, not ever. That's what it means to me.

Quentin Bryce, former Governor-General of Australia,
the first woman to hold that office

Part One

THE SPEECH

Chapter 1

Personal reflections on the misogyny speech

Julia Gillard

Sliding doors, transformative moments: whatever you call them, life can be shaped by a few pivotal decisions.

Often the importance of the decision is clear at the time. Should I move far away from everything I have known, leave my current comfortable job and jump to something new, should I commit to this partner, have children, buy this house . . . and the list goes on.

Sometimes, though, the significance of a decision is only clear in retrospect. Such is the case for a previously untold part of the story of the misogyny speech, something I had forgotten until I was preparing this collection of essays.

That there was an aspect of the day of which I had no memory truly shocked me. Because I am often asked about the misogyny speech, I have frequently recalled the circumstances of that parliamentary day to mind. I have always viewed my memories as sharp. I can close my eyes and see in my mind scenes from the day. I can summon the feelings of the moment.

Yet, a part of the story had been lost to me and, as a result of this book, it has now been rediscovered. I want to share it with you, but in order for it to make sense I first need to paint a picture of the day the misogyny speech was delivered, 9 October 2012.

Core to understanding the day is familiarity with the rhythms of parliament, especially the House of Representatives, which on the day of the misogyny speech comprised 150 members.

The procedures of the Australian parliament are modelled on the United Kingdom parliament in Westminster. When the British arrived to dump convicts and colonise the continent, beginning the long and painful history of dispossession and discrimination against First Nations people, they brought with them their template for creating parliaments.

When the colonies became states and came together as a nation, it was inevitable the federal parliament would be modelled on Westminster. Consequently, every sitting day in the House includes the Westminster ritual of Question Time. Everything from the green colour scheme in the chamber to the fact that Question Time is the most noted and theatrical part of the day can be traced back to Britain.

But there are significant local adaptations. Our Question Time starts at 2 pm each day, and questions can be asked on any topic to any minister. The prime minister is expected to be in Question Time every day and almost inevitably is asked a disproportionate share of the questions.

These are Australian innovations. In the United Kingdom, the prime minister only comes to Question Time once a week and other daily question times are themed, with a particular minister in the firing line. For example, one Question Time might be all about education, with the Minister for Education in the hot seat.

There is also paperwork involved, with a requirement for questions to be filed in advance and disseminated on the notice paper. The use of supplementary questions means that, despite these rules, many questions are effectively given without notice. However, this is still a contrast to the Australian system, where no notice is given of the questions that will be asked.

The ferocity of the proceedings is also uniquely our own. While Westminster Question Time is full of cheering, jeering and snide remarks, in the Australian parliament we have more fully weaponised proceedings, with blunt force personal insults. Visiting politicians from the United Kingdom who sit in the gallery to watch the local display usually walk away stunned.

In both places, party politics and media reporting have also changed Question Time from its historic roots. Originally envisaged as an opportunity for the opposition and backbenchers to hold executive government to account by asking questions, this is now just one element of proceedings. When a scandal is afoot and the questioning is forensic, accountability is at the fore of proceedings. Occasionally a backbencher will ask a genuinely local question focused on whether a government minister is considering the needs of their electorate fairly. However, Question Time today is overwhelmingly a kind of rhetorical theatre made for television, which is unsurprising given it is shown on free-to-air TV every day. The opposition's aim is to put the government under political pressure and have that taken up by news reports. Often no real pressure is generated, but a lot of flamboyant, media-savvy lines are embedded in the questions asked. Meanwhile, the government is endeavouring to defuse any attack and get its own sound bites in the news about the government's agenda or the weakness of the opposition.

The questions asked are carefully calibrated by each side, and the stories running in the media that day are at the centre of everyone's tactical calculations. Often by early morning, as a result of the morning newspapers, breakfast television, radio and social media, it is pretty clear what is the emerging political story of the day.

For the opposition, capitalising on this story through Question Time is easier than trying to get a whole new narrative running. Indeed, journalists might well be pressing, nodding and winking that questions which take a particular tack and are aligned with the current media interest will get a good run.

All this means the government can make a highly informed guess about the likely line of questioning, at least for the first four or five of the nine or ten questions the opposition will have time to ask before the Question Time session is brought to a close. In addition to preparing defensively, the government has to decide on what themes it wants to push in the questions its own back-benchers will ask.

My parliamentary days included many obligations such as Cabinet and other formal government meetings, individual meetings with parliamentarians or external stakeholders, events, media conferences, a mountain of paperwork and so on. The hours were long, with the House itself regularly sitting from morning to late in the night, and work expectations well exceeded these formal hours.

While each day differed from the one before in many respects, the one constancy would be getting ready for Question Time. Our tactics committee would meet first thing in the morning to decide the themes for the day. These discussions would be reported to me, and a further mull over what was the best approach would occur.

After these initial meetings, someone had to write the actual questions and prepare the defensive briefing notes. For me, the two people at the centre of that process were Andrew Downes, one of my political advisers who on parliamentary days specialised in this work, and Ben Hubbard, my chief of staff. In the political calculations and preparatory work, the advice and expertise of key media and policy staff were also relied on.

By late morning, a second tactics committee meeting would be held to sign off on the questions. I would have my final briefing with staff in the middle of the day and then work on my own for the hour or so before Question Time to absorb the material.

Of course, this all makes it sound more methodical than the process often was. One of the things that makes politics both hard and fascinating is its unpredictability. Many were the days on which decisions carefully made at the early morning meeting were upended because a true drama or even a modest kerfuffle happened just before 2 pm. This could be anything from a major international development to someone making a stupid gaffe in a media interview. In an instant, the story of the day and the likely questions would shift, and work at a frantic pace was required to adjust.

No doubt each day as I was doing this work in my office, the opposition, led by Tony Abbott, was going through similar processes to work out the questions they would ask.

Once settled, the questions are distributed in writing to those who will ask them. For the opposition, the attack questions are usually asked by the leader or shadow ministers. For the government, the softball questions, designed to enable the prime minister or a minister to wax lyrical about the government's achievements and its superiority to the opposition, are allocated to backbenchers.

Perhaps somewhat oddly, in Australia this category of deliberately planted questions is called a Dorothy Dixer, or just a Dixer, named for an American advice columnist who wrote under the pen-name Dorothy Dix. At the time of her death in 1951 she was the most widely read female journalist in the world, with her columns syndicated to an audience of more than 50 million readers. The reference is made because it was rumoured that she herself wrote some of the questions she answered in her column, to give her the opportunity to address a certain topic. (However, given that throughout her long life she also campaigned for women's suffrage and wrote on other feminist causes, this rumour could well be the kind of undermining attack on a star-performing activist woman that still happens today.)

In so many ways, the day of the misogyny speech started out the same as other parliamentary days. It was a Tuesday, the morning of which is always devoted to party room meetings. Before I went to our Labor caucus meeting, our tactics discussions began. On this day there was no mistaking the likely theme of Question Time. It was clearly going to be all about the fact that on the previous day, Monday, court documents had become public which detailed deeply sexist text messages that had been sent by the then Speaker of the House of Representatives, Peter Slipper.

Under normal circumstances, the Speaker sits above the political fray. The Speaker is elected by members of the House, and that usually means the government can use its majority to ensure the Speaker is one of their own. As a balancing factor, one Deputy Speaker is drawn from the opposition party and there is a broader group selected to share the duties of being Speaker. With the long parliamentary hours and the degree of concentration necessary to keep the proceedings running smoothly and in order, it is necessary to have a group of people who can share the load. However, it is the Speaker's responsibility to sit in the chair for Question Time, the hardest and most unruly session of the day.

Notwithstanding which political party they come from, anyone undertaking the duties of Speaker is supposed to act fairly and impartially.

For the government I led, things were a little different, because we governed with the support of independents and the Greens. Without having a majority in our own right, it was not necessarily so simple as deciding who we wanted to sit in the Speaker's chair. However, when the government was first elected, there was no opposition to Harry Jenkins, a Labor Member of Parliament, continuing as Speaker. He had served in that role prior to the election and was well respected by all. One of his deputies, Peter Slipper, was drawn from the Liberal Party. Anna Burke, from the Labor Party, was also elected as a deputy.

A minority government like the one I led has all the usual pressures of governing well, plus the extra weight of not being able to assume that the numbers are automatically there to pass legislation or win procedural motions in the House. It takes care and attention every time to make sure a vote will be won. During the days of my government, we were incredibly successful at winning through, passing more than five hundred bills and taking the record as the most productive parliament in Australian history. However, we were always thinking about what would make this task easier.

An opportunity to change the numbers in our favour presented itself in late 2011. By then, it was clear that Peter Slipper, who held the Queensland seat of Fairfax, was increasingly disaffected with the Liberal Party, which looked set to endorse someone else to stand as the Liberal candidate in his electorate for the next election. The likely replacement was Mal Brough, who had served as a Cabinet minister in John Howard's government. He had lost his seat in the 2007 election and was keen to re-enter parliament. With this background, if nominated as Speaker, Slipper would serve.

On the last day of the 2011 parliamentary year, Harry Jenkins resigned as Speaker. In his own words:

> As members are aware in this the 43rd parliament, to further avoid controversial party political matters I have divorced myself from involvement with the federal parliamentary Labor Party. In this era of minority government I have pro- gressively become frustrated at this stricture. My desire is to be able to participate in policy and parliamentary debate, and this would be incompatible with continuing in the role of Speaker.

The government nominated and supported Peter Slipper to take his place. On the basis of his work as Deputy Speaker, we thought he would perform the role competently and, by taking a vote from the opposition and adding Harry back into Labor's parliamentary ranks, his election would increase our security on the floor of the parliament. In taking up the role, Slipper resigned from the Liberal Party, which reacted ferociously to what it viewed as his betrayal.

During the course of 2012, Peter Slipper became involved in two scandals. One related to misuse of parliamentary entitlements. The other attracted more public attention and stemmed from his media adviser, James Ashby, commencing legal proceedings against Slipper relating to sexual harassment.

Over the years that followed there were a number of aftershocks from these events. The Australian Federal Police investigated whether a group of Liberal Party parliamentarians had been involved in inducing Ashby to make his allegations against Peter Slipper or in illegally obtaining, through him, Slipper's diary. James Ashby went on to work for Pauline Hanson, leader of the One Nation Party.

But all of that lay in the future. On that Tuesday, I felt as if I was trying to find my footing in a pounding sea of sexism, misogyny and hypocrisy.

Certainly, Peter Slipper needed to resign as Speaker. Court processes were in train to determine the various allegations against him, and in April 2012 he had stood aside while those processes were worked through. But the sexism that had now been revealed was unambiguous and undenied. Slipper had acknowledged he was the author of the text messages. I knew he had to go, and that was the view of key independents in the parliament who had supported his initial election as Speaker. Over the course of the day he came to accept he had no choice but to resign, and he did so a few hours after the end of Question Time.

However, to say it stuck in my throat that the opposition was now claiming furious concern about sexism is a woeful under-statement. I was gagging on the hypocrisy.

Throughout my prime ministership, gendered imagery and insults had surrounded me, continually spewed out by the opposition, shock jocks, sections of the media and some in the world of business, to name just a few.

The imagery deliberately drawn around me was that of a ruthless and unnatural woman who had clawed her way to power, lacked the human instinct to have children, and was incapable of caring for others and understanding the love of family. Bitch, witch, menopausal monster, that my father had died of shame – I had heard it all. The same opposition that was now claiming it was deeply offended at the sexism of text messages containing crude references to female genitalia had revelled in throwing misogynistic muck at me day after day.

As extra icing on this stinking hypocrisy cake, it was clear the opposition was going to slam me as someone who was supporting a misogynist, even though I could not have known about the text messages when the government nominated Peter Slipper to become Speaker. Indeed, the messages were authored while Slipper was one of the opposition's number, not the Speaker.

As I said in my memoir, *My Story*, I do not normally think in swearwords, but my internal monologue was shouting, *For fuck's sake, after all the shit I have put up with, now I have to listen to Abbott lecturing me on sexism. For fuck's sake!*

This angry frustration was predominantly directed at the opposition, but a dose of it was also directed at myself. Predictably, part of that was about having supported Slipper for the Speaker role. But an even bigger part was about how I had mishandled the issues of sexism and misogyny during my time as prime minister. I had failed to speak up when I should have. I ought to have taken on these issues early in my term, when the opposition first advanced such gendered critiques and when the media first treated me demonstrably differently.

It was not fear that had held me back from taking up the cudgels. After all, I was in an empowered and privileged position. Rather, it was because I had misjudged, thinking that the longer I governed and the more everyone became used to a woman in the lead political role, the more the sexism would fall away. I had thought I didn't need to fight it or call it out; I simply had to live through it.

And live through it I had. Not flinching, trying not to take it to heart, pushing through. But all that effortful resilience had got me was everyone doubling down on the gendered critiques, and now I had landed in this weird world where, having smiled and ignored so much sexism directed at me, I was now the one being accused of it.

It was beyond maddening, almost beyond belief.

Yet, at another level, for a parliamentary day it was business as usual. The opposition was going to come at me and the government hard, using whatever ammunition they could muster, and that was all there was to it.

Given the nature of the likely attack, it was not a day that needed extensive and complicated preparation. If the theme of the day had been a concerted takedown of a government policy or its implementation, then we might have needed to pull out all stops to gather the evidence together in a quick and digestible form, so that any allegations of failure could be immediately countered.

But what this day called for was material that would demonstrate the opposition was just politically posturing, and not seriously concerned about sexism. That their righteous anger was confected and, while the issues that surrounded Slipper as Speaker did need to be resolved, the opposition was not really interested in finding a solution.

I therefore asked my team to pull together around ten of Tony Abbott's most sexist quotes, which I intended to use in reply when he asked me questions, in order to show his hypocrisy.

Subsequently I have joked that, from the point of view of my hard-working staff, the preparation task I asked them to complete that day was not an onerous one. Finding the quotes was easy.

From today's vantage point, the comparative lack of drama in this part of the day looks to me like an eerie calm before the misogyny speech storm. But at the time, I had no sense of that. I knew I would have to push back forcefully in Question Time, but holding my own in that combative parliamentary theatre was by no means new to me.

I know for many Australians, and particularly for many women, the rudeness and roar of Question Time puts them off politics. Some assume that every parliamentary hour is like that, whereas the truth is that many are spent quietly processing new laws about which everyone is in agreement, or calmly debating proposals on which people differ. That it is Question Time that creates the sport of the day and dominates the news coverage can give a very false impression.

Even those who recognise it's not always like that cannot imagine themselves participating in a world where such behaviour is tolerated and even rewarded. I fully understand and respect this view, and think it is inevitable that there will be major parliamentary procedural reform at some point. Electors are increasingly demanding that they see a parliament that works civilly, in which a new kind of politics is at play.

But for me, entering the parliament in 1998, one of the things I wanted to do was to show a woman could thrive in, indeed dominate, the proceedings in the parliamentary chamber. I brought with me debating skills honed at school, in student and Labor politics, and in my time working in the law. I was determined to give as good as I got, and I delighted in performing roles such as Manager of

Opposition Business in the House, which put me at the centre of the parliamentary action.

That all meant that by the time I was prime minister, I was experienced in holding my own and winning through when it got tough.

As the hour of Question Time rolled around, I felt ready. My angry frustration had burnt itself out and left behind it a cool anger. I was calm and felt in the zone.

The walk from the prime minister's office to the House of Representatives takes a few minutes, including walking through a glass corridor as you approach the double doors leading to the House. On many days, while taking this walk, I could feel the exact moment my adrenaline kicked in, giving me a jolt for the contest to come. Sometimes, alongside that jolt, I could hear my heartbeat in my ears.

On this day, I felt settled, loose limbed. I entered the House and saw Anna Burke in the Speaker's chair and the opposition in their seats, ready for action.

The day started with a predictable question from Tony Abbott about whether I still had confidence in Peter Slipper as Speaker. I answered, and then the proceedings took an unpredictable turn. A very common rhythm to Question Time was the opposition pounding away on its attack for six or seven or eight questions, and then the Leader of the Opposition would move to suspend standing orders to allow debate on a motion censuring the government for whatever issue was at the centre of the attack.

Parliament's daily work is defined by what appears on the circulated notice paper. Suspending standing orders simply means that predetermined order of business is put aside to allow a new debate to be brought on. In the past, this tactic had been used quite sparely by oppositions and reserved for the most serious matters. However, the Abbott Opposition had made it part of its stock strategies and did it frequently. Even in a parliament where the government did not have a majority, the motion to suspend standing orders would never get carried. Actually *winning* the vote on the motion was not the point. The very moving of the motion triggered a debate and allowed the opposition, especially Tony Abbott, a chance to get their attack lines out.

As routine as this strategy was, it really was very odd for this to happen only minutes into Question Time, immediately after the first question.

Because of the overuse by the opposition of this approach of triggering a procedural debate, my general policy was not to be the government speaker who replied to them. I and the tactics committee were of the view that me being involved would bring me down to the opposition leader's level. Instead, Abbott would speak first, and a senior government speaker, often Anthony Albanese, who was our chief point person as Leader of the House, would speak in reply. At the end of the debate, a vote would be called and that would be the end of it.

What my former chief of staff, Ben Hubbard, reminded me of as I was preparing this book, the part that I had completely forgotten, is that I didn't just settle in to deliver the parliamentary reply as soon as Abbott was on his feet. Ben, along with Andrew Downes, sat during each Question Time on the floor of the parliament in the advisers' box. It is a privilege accorded to few staff members. In Ben's words, 'The advisers' box on the floor provides a position in among the players but oddly detached.' Of that day, he recalls:

During Question Time, Abbott moved a procedural motion and used it as an opportunity to bluster. It was a standard tactic for him: try to create chaos and distraction mixed with full-throated machismo.

When the PM came over to inform us that she was going to take the government response, I was surprised. She'd typically stayed above these tactics, so I asked, 'Are you sure?' She considered my question.

I have no memory of this exchange, or of ever reconsidering the question as to whether I should be the one to reply. Imagine if I had rethought and decided to say no. The misogyny speech would never have been delivered.

But Ben is clear in his recollection that my moment of reflection was not long. He says:

But then the PM said she was 'sick of this shit'. The visible wilting of the opposition frontbench in the subsequent minutes showed I needn't have been worried.

In the time this exchange was taking place, Anthony – always called Albo by his friends, and now being referred to in that way by the entire nation he leads as prime minister – was making arrangements to move this from a procedural debate to a substantive one. As a result, more people would have an opportunity to speak, but this was always going to be seen as a head-to-head clash between me and Tony Abbott.

While he spoke, as the first of the opposition's speakers, I listened with one ear while gathering my thoughts and jotting down dot-point notes that would remind me of the key arguments

I wanted to make. My handwriting is dreadful, illegible often. Even I can struggle to decipher it. But this was very few scribbles on a sheet of paper. Somehow I knew the words would come out of my mouth when I needed them to, and they did.

When I rose as the first speaker for the government it was to a wall of noise, mostly coming from the opposition but some of it supporting interjections from my own side. Out flowed the speech, and I knew as I was delivering it that the words were powerful. The opposition went from yelling at me to getting quieter, then to dropping their heads and looking at their phones. Famously, Tony Abbott looked at his watch and I wrapped that into the speech, noting it as a mark of disrespect.

Then it was done. After staying silent, I'd had my say. At no time did I feel worked up or hotly angry. I felt strong, measured, controlled. Yet emotion did play its role in the energy of the speech. The frustration that sexism and misogyny could still be so bad in the twenty-first century. The toll of not pointing it out. The fact that the topic of sexism was seen as a political plaything for use in a Question Time attack when it suited and then forgotten about immediately after.

And there was another chord of emotion, too. At one point in his opening speech, Tony Abbott said:

> every day the Prime Minister stands in this parliament to defend this Speaker will be another day of shame for this parliament and another day of shame for a government which should have already died of shame.

These words echoed the disgusting comments made by the conservative radio shock jock Alan Jones, who in September 2012, not long after my father's death, thought that it would be funny to joke at a Sydney University Liberal Club dinner that 'The old man recently died a few weeks ago of shame. To think that he had a daughter who told lies every time she stood for parliament.'

As if that was not vile enough, at the same event the club auctioned off a jacket made of chaff bags and autographed by Alan Jones. This was meant as comic memorabilia of Jones's prior declaration that I should be 'put into a chaff bag and thrown into the sea'.

In the years since the misogyny speech I have had many women, especially conservative business leaders, express to me surprise and dismay about the treatment of women by the Australian Liberal Party. My response has always been to empathise and discuss potential strategies for change. Yet even while I was having one of these conversations, in the back of my mind I would be trying to process why anyone would be surprised. Surely, after watching my time in office and seeing the way the Liberal Party conducted itself on gender, it should be completely obvious to everyone that this was an organisation steeped in sexism.

On the day of the misogyny speech, Abbott's channelling, even subconsciously, of Alan Jones's words spurred me on.

When the speech was over, I resumed my seat in parliament and the next speaker began. I knew I would have to sit until the end of the debate but there was no need for me to listen intently to the remaining speeches.

I felt calm, not spent. I spun my chair around to Wayne Swan, the deputy prime minister, and suggested to him that I might ask the advisers to have my correspondence basket run in so I could work through some letters while the motion was further discussed. Wayne said, with force and urgency, 'You can't give the *j'accuse* speech and then start looking at paperwork.' Let me assure you, Wayne is not the kind of person who regularly bursts into speaking in French. What he felt, which at that moment I did not, was that this was a speech which would resonate and have the force of denunciation that is evoked by the term *j'accuse*.

Taking a break from his task of moving around the chamber and helping to prepare the next speakers, Albo sat with me momentarily and joked he had felt sorry for Abbott when he looked at his watch. Here was another indication the speech had packed a mighty punch.

When the debate was over and the motion moved by the opposition was defeated, I walked up to the advisers' box and did the same thing I always did at the end of Question Time: I gave Andrew Downes my briefing folder and my handwritten notes. I never wanted to leave anything on the table in the House for the opposition to find. Andrew must have had some inkling that the speech would live on, because he kept the notes rather than shredding them, which is what he usually would have done.

I walked back to my office, ready to get on with the rest of the day's work. Later in the day, Peter Slipper resigned, events moved on as they do in politics and, as always, there was more to do. More paperwork, more meetings, more people to meet.

Even as I was taking those steps back to my desk, my speech, what is now known as 'the misogyny speech', was starting to make its way to women around the world. I am amazed and delighted that ten years later it still has meaning as a rallying cry.

For me, it is now integrated into who I am and how I am perceived. When I travel internationally, I end up meeting many women and some men who want to talk to me about the misogyny speech. It is often the only thing they know about me, and sometimes the one contact point they have with Australian politics. I meet women in Australia and around the world who tell me about watching the speech dozens, if not hundreds, of times.

The huge degree of focus on the speech used to cause me some concern. I would think to myself that, after fifteen years in politics, three as deputy prime minister and three as prime minister, it was a bit odd that your career would be condensed to one short speech.

But I am reconciled with that now and proud the speech lives on. Indeed, for me, the speech lives in two moments in time. It is in my memory as part of my past. While I have been replayed snippets of the speech when I have been interviewed about it, I have never sat down and watched it in full, and I do not think I ever will. I want my memory to be about how it felt to deliver the speech and what I saw through my eyes. I do not want that overlaid by the different view given by the film footage.

More importantly, though, the speech is present in my contemporary work. It is a calling card that has helped me push for a deepening of dialogue and research about women and leadership. It is now a springboard to more evidence and more action in the pursuit of gender equality. That is the work of the Global Institute for Women's Leadership, of which I serve as chair, and it is the spirit in which this volume of essays is offered to you.

We cannot change the past, but the past can inspire us to campaign and change the future. My most sincere hope is for that to be the ongoing role of the misogyny speech.

(1) $\longrightarrow$ Microscopy + its consequences,
       look of the apparatus.

(2) Stokesels against even
    diagnostic nunreachen.
    $\longrightarrow$ explain the
    $\longrightarrow$

(3) Woken up — millissecs
    look in the mirror.

(4) Slipper — perinal food.
    enjoyed his support —

(5) Standed / Slipper —
    _____

    Sed palace —
    Coy perturolia — vile fish,
                         _____
                    Extenc Issue
                         ____

(1) Miso
    – statements against can
      disquali.. his office.

    statements →

(2) Responsibilis | conduct
    f~ other.   →   styles Yeng
                          disvoll.

(3) Support.   Responsil..

(4) Buller

    *   →   Shame.

              →   Uras.

Julia Gillard's handwritten notes for the misogyny speech

As Julia pulled Tony Abbott apart limb from limb I thought, *How gutsy is this!* He'd had this coming.

With barely a note in hand, Julia smashed into his sexism, dishonesty, double standards and unfitness for office.

She was on fire!

And then she sat down as if nothing extraordinary had happened, and said to me she was going to get on with a bit of paperwork.

I looked at her and said, 'You've got to be kidding. You can't do that – you've just given the *j'accuse* speech.' That timeless statement of political justice is remembered more than a century later for its mixture of penetrating, forensic analysis and controlled anger. I recognised immediately that Julia had just delivered a speech with those same qualities, and that historians would be writing about it for years to come.

Wayne Swan, National President of the Australian Labor Party and former Deputy Prime Minister of Australia

Chapter 2

In the media: Reporting on gender and the misogyny speech

Katharine Murphy

I was nervous about looking back at the words I wrote on 9 October 2012. I didn't think my reporting would be terrible, I just doubted I'd be proud of it. Back then, my primary job was live-blogging federal politics. *The Age*, the broadsheet newspaper I worked for at the time, was transforming itself into a digital-first news agency. The transition was brutal. There was mass shedding of jobs as the internet blew a hole in our business models. Journalists wondered what journalism actually was in this new age, and there were turf wars going on inside Fairfax Media, the organisation that owned *The Age*, as the newspaper and digital arms were integrated.

Live reporting was a refuge from those existential uncertainties. In that mode, I covered parliament in ten- or fifteen-minute intervals, sometimes posting for twelve hours at a time. We were making up this style of reporting as we went. Readers had a voracious appetite for news as it happened, and we were trying to migrate the old newspaper values to live reportage in the new world. None of this scene-setting is an excuse, it's just context. I'm scoping out my professional milieu as I sat, plugged in to the matrix, and listened to Julia Gillard hurling the words that became the misogyny speech – a set of words powerful enough to travel around the world.

That day in the 43rd Parliament was much like all the others. Labor governed in minority and every day was a struggle. My first post on the live blog that day was at 9.30 am. This was a late start because I'd been out watching Gillard at a breakfast event outside the parliament. My last post on the blog that day was at 10.35 pm. We'll get to the specifics of the day shortly, but first, some background about the 43rd Parliament. The Gillard government lacked a majority in both chambers, but it had an ambitious policy agenda that it pursued relentlessly through the roller-coaster of contested party leadership. As Labor legislated a carbon price, paid parental leave and a National Disability Insurance Scheme, Kevin Rudd was on track to return to the prime ministership he had lost in 2010. While the government slogged forward, battling in what felt like a game of inches, the endorphin-charged opposition leader, Tony Abbott, intent on victory, engineered a daily sense of crisis in the parliament.

Abbott was a creature of institutions – Riverview school, Oxford, the seminary, the Liberal Party – and understood how to harness their power. Federal parliament was his playground. The pugilistic sound stage suited him. He moved near-daily suspensions of the standing orders – a procedure used to disrupt the parliamentary program – to create a palpable sense that the Gillard government was teetering on the edge of collapse. Abbott was expert at cueing Australia's right-wing media – the Rupert Murdoch–owned metropolitan tabloids, the national broadsheet

The Australian, the 'just us blokes' zone of talkback radio – and he used the content-hungry white-water news cycle to amplify a governance crisis he fomented with ferocious precision.

On the day of the misogyny speech, the Speaker of the House of Representatives, Peter Slipper, was embroiled in a serious controversy. Labor had wooed Slipper, a Liberal MP, to the Speaker's chair in an effort to bolster its control of the chamber. On that day in October, Abbott had put forward a motion to have Slipper removed as the Speaker. This followed the release of crude text messages Slipper had sent to a former adviser, James Ashby. The messages had surfaced as evidence in a sexual harassment case Ashby had launched against Slipper. Abbott was again on the offensive. The Speaker had 'failed the character test', he thundered in parliament, adding that Gillard had 'failed the judgement test' by appointing him as a presiding officer.

Shame was Abbott's rhetorical weapon of choice. 'Should *she* ['she' being the prime minister] now rise in this place to try to defend the Speaker, to say that she retains confidence in the Speaker, she will shame this parliament again,' Abbott said. 'And every day the Prime Minister stands in this parliament to defend this Speaker will be another day of shame for this parliament and another day of shame for a government which should have already died of shame.'

I said before that *shame* was Abbott's preferred rhetorical weapon, but it was not just his. A mate of the opposition leader's, the Sydney radio shock jock Alan Jones, had contended just a few weeks earlier that Gillard's late father, John, had 'died of shame' because of his daughter's political 'lies' – slander he later had to walk back. At the same event where Jones sprayed this bile, a chaff bag signed by him was also auctioned off. This particular curio was a reference to an earlier observation from Jones that Gillard should be put into a chaff bag and thrown out to sea. Treachery was the trope of choice; Gillard's behaviour, from the infamous empty fruit bowl, to taking the Labor leadership from Rudd rather than waiting for her turn, was unwomanly and therefore worthy of condemnation. The language deployed by the phalanx of Gillard haters was like a relay: ad hominem passed hand to hand and conveyed up the field.

Abbott said nothing of his own shame, or the Liberal Party's shame by association, for having preselected Slipper to stand as a Queensland representative election after election. In the past, Abbott had attended Slipper's wedding and referred to him as a friend. Abbott's hypocrisy hovered thick in the air. We could all see it, but it was measured by the self-exonerating yardsticks of politics and the rampant 'both sides-ism' that is deep-etched in political journalism. In the way of politics, Abbott's hypocrisy both mattered and did not matter, because the default mode is that everyone in politics is capable of self-serving behaviour. Politics is built on fair-weather friendships, shifting alliances and transactional betrayal. That's the sand on which the vocation stands, and, periodically, sinks. So, reporters focused on the nuts and bolts of another huge day. Would Slipper survive as Speaker? Would this uproar spiral into a confidence vote? Would the Gillard government be shaken to its core? In the moment – and the 24/7 media cycle is all about the moment – this question felt important. Crucial, even.

Bear in mind the Hansard to this day records Gillard's now-iconic remarks perfunctorily as 'Motions' – 'Speaker' – 'Speech'. My head was in those things – motions, speaker, speech – in the minutiae of parliament. The procedure I was documenting live was a series of moves on a chessboard, moves I'd been trained to witness and report with clinical detachment. Of course, I heard Gillard's words of rebuttal – which is what the misogyny speech was, a rebuttal of Abbott and his motion against Slipper. I appreciated Gillard's concision, her melodic repetitions, *I will not*; the fierce intelligence of a professional advocate informing yet another parliamentary improvisation. I glimpsed the white-hot anger she'd kept leashed behind a visage of ironic detachment during her prime ministership. On that day, during that hour, in those moments, Gillard thrummed like an Exocet missile. At 2.45 pm I posted on my live blog: *The Prime Minister's voice is shaking. Rage? Nerves? Both?*

Gillard was always brutal in parliament; withering and droll. The misogyny speech wasn't some rhetorical bolt from the blue, it was the apotheosis of long practised lawyerly and parliamentary technique. It's likely I cheered privately, in my mind, at some of her turns of phrase. I'm reasonably confident I did. I recall Wayne Swan's face – a flicker of unease, I thought, because Swan often looked anxious in those anxious times, but perhaps it was admiration – as Gillard unleashed rhetorical blow after rhetorical blow. I also recall studying Abbott's face as he watched Gillard skewer him across the despatch box. At first, the opposition leader looked entirely pleased with himself. Later, a shadow of something – not remorse, obviously, that's too much, but something – self-awareness, perhaps? In any case, the impulse was quickly suppressed.

Gillard was fighting for her prime ministership, for her dignity, for her reputation, for fair treatment, for a measure of respect. This was an epic battle requiring inhuman levels of fortitude. It seems bizarre to me now how much we discounted that fact, how much we took her stoicism for granted, almost as if it were something we and the voting public were owed. We discounted it because

Gillard did that most days. That's one of the reasons we, the journalists who wrote the first draft of history on that day, missed the cultural power of the contribution, or, rather, looked through it. We discounted the essence of the speech because we were creatures of the Canberra cloisters. We were mired in those intrigues, masters of that environment, striving always for perfect fluency, for the authoritative translation. Our theatre of battle was intraday politics, and intraday politics was a battle Australia's first female prime minister was losing.

•

I arrived in the parliamentary press gallery in 1996. When I chose to have my first child a couple of years later, in my late twenties, with little professional status to speak of, colleagues told me I was finished. Back then, women in my line of work waited to have their children until they were well established in the newsroom hierarchy. Having negligible status in the hierarchy plus caring responsibilities seemed rash to some of my contemporaries – a life choice that hovered somewhere between eccentric and professional harakiri. In contemporary terms, in the age of paid parental leave, this sensibility might sound harsh or unreconstructed, but the workplace culture of my first decade in journalism was actually benign, at least in the places I worked. Nobody hit on me or talked over the top of me, but nobody was encouraged to see their own humanity, or, in my case, their own female perspective, obligations or experiences, as being in any way relevant to the task at hand.

When I suffered from crippling morning sickness during my first pregnancy, a male colleague told me in an authoritative tone that managing my symptoms was predominantly a mind game.

I just needed to find my internal equilibrium and I would stop vomiting around the clock. When I came back to work after having my second child and asked not to be the chief of staff in the bureau where I was then stationed so I could periodically see my babies before they slept, the bosses in Sydney made it clear that wasn't possible. I was expected to make it work. Instead, I moved to another newspaper and a new job with no management responsibilities – which was probably what my superiors hoped I would do, so the bureau would be spared the inconvenience of my parental responsibilities.

Again, these experiences sound primitive, but the environment wasn't terrible. As a young political journalist, I was surrounded by women who had managed to advance in parliamentary press gallery journalism – the most competitive media precinct in the country. I didn't lack role models. Nobody of my acquaintance was ambivalent about being a feminist. We were the grateful beneficiaries of decades of progress.

But politics, my professional ecosystem, remained predominantly a male theatre. The 'voice of God' journalistic style of that era also sounded white, middle-aged and male. The women who had clambered to the top of the journalism heap weren't writing as women, they were writing as the equal of men in the dispassionate, detached, analytical style of our craft. The accrued life experience of women – the casual sexism, predations and, too often, sexual violence – wasn't something we projected into our writing. There was no male newsroom overlord or tone policeman forbidding a female perspective and erasing any trace of it from copy, but news writing was a formula that anonymised gender.

In the culture in which I was hewn, there were serious journalists, gun news-breakers and erudite columnists, both male and female, and then there were women who wrote about their kids or wrote about 'women's issues'. I cannot ever remember reflecting during that formative period in my professional life about whether my gender was relevant to the subjects at hand, or whether it might furnish a useful perspective or insight. What would being a woman tell you about covering the waterfront dispute, or tax reform, or Indigenous land rights, or climate change, or trade agreements? Nothing. Or so we thought.

When Gillard came to power, I celebrated that achievement like most Australian women. Her ascendancy seemed both remarkable and the natural way of things. As it should and must be. When the toxicity started, and it started almost immediately – Lady Macbeth, Ditch the witch, Bob Brown's bitch; the oversized focus on the wardrobe, the earlobes, the hairdresser boyfriend, the chaff bag, the 'small breasts, huge thighs' and 'big red box', the 'big arse' – I looked through the torrent of sexism and misogyny as one would survey a distant object shrouded in fog. Present in the line of sight, but somehow obscured.

Obviously all this was grotesque – an unreconstructed, gendered beat-down that could have only happened with cultural impunity in the pre-#MeToo era. The sexism Australia's first female prime minister faced certainly wasn't lost on me. I called it out periodically. I was so enraged by the allegedly comic *At Home with Julia* satire that aired on the ABC in 2011, I sought some column inches in my newspaper to let rip.

But on some level, I couldn't process what was happening. I couldn't fathom it. I understood that male entitlement remained a cultural default, but the male entitlement informing the gratuitous critique of Gillard's looks, idioms and character by some of her political opponents, and some Neanderthal media figures, undermined truths about progress that I believed to be absolute. Without ever being particularly conscious of this being a decision, or an active accommodation I was making, I minimised the whole phenomenon in my mind. Most of the time, I put any evidence that felt too awful to process aside, into a box.

Periodically, I unlocked the box and interrogated its contents. I coached myself to look beyond what was very obviously in front of me. This visceral backlash had to be more complicated than the fact Gillard was a woman occupying space that a man thought was rightfully his. Obviously, Australia's 27th prime minister had her flaws, like every other occupant of the office. Being prime minister is a tough job. Every stumble is magnified, nobody thanks you for being competent. There were the contested circumstances of Gillard obtaining the leadership: regicidal conditions that gave licence to loaded rhetoric such as 'treachery' and 'shame'. Back when I was a teenager, Richard Carleton had asked Bob Hawke whether he felt 'a little embarrassed tonight at the blood that's on your hands' in a famous television interview after Hawke took the leadership of the Labor Party from Bill Hayden. In the same genre, when Gillard took the leadership from Rudd, Julia Irwin, a Labor MP, commented, 'Not since Brutus stabbed Julius Caesar have we seen such an act of betrayal.' Politics was a tough business, robust criticism was an equal-opportunity sport, and Gillard had proven herself the toughest of all – tough enough to move Rudd out of his prime ministerial office because a 'good government had lost its way'.

So, it was complicated, genuinely, and not just for me. Having sought to be a prime minister for all Australians, Gillard clearly did not want to style herself as a feminist martyr or as the prime minister for women. That would have gratified her enemies, leached energy from her prime ministership and stranded her in the cul-de-sac no professional woman wants to be in – the one where you are defined exclusively by your gender. I suspect many of Gillard's female contemporaries in the Labor Party felt the same sort of cognitive dissonance and internal conflicts as I did, and so bit their tongues.

But it was there. It was always there. That persistent undercurrent of animosity, of fury directed at a woman who had the temerity to silence male power in the highest office in the land.

Good women are supposed to be ambivalent about power; to ask for it nicely, with charm, not force.

Nice girls don't carry knives.[1]

•

Gillard has described the misogyny speech as 'a crack point'. In September 2013, only months after leaving the prime ministership, she said: 'I thought after everything I have experienced, I have to listen to Tony Abbott lecture me about sexism . . . That gave me the emotional start to the speech and once I started, it took on a life of its own.'[2] A couple of years ago, Ben Rhodes, a former adviser to Barack Obama, confessed that presidential staff used to fire up the video of the speech at points when the administration was angry or frustrated with Tony Abbott in their dealings with him as prime minister. 'That speech got watched a lot in the Obama White House, let me just put it that way,' Rhodes said in 2020.[3]

For me, the speech is the Gillard prime ministership in microcosm. It showcases her fundamental capabilities, and the institutional limits she pressed up against from the moment she took the job. And the thing about the Gillard prime ministership is, it picked me up and set me down in a different place.

I'm sure many Australian women had the same experience: the same forced recalibration of the notions of equality, and progress. When Gillard left office, I was more disconcerted than angry, more alive than I ever had been previously to pernicious structures of silencing. Political journalists are fascinated by power. We parse it in all its forms. We develop mud maps of institutions to better understand how power is allocated and exercised between groups and individuals. After Gillard, I understood that one of the relevant power dynamics to interrogate in Canberra was gender.

Once lived experience validated gender as a line of interrogation, problems surfaced everywhere. I saw it when Abbott's former chief of staff, Peta Credlin, another political woman who refused to conform or defer, was castigated for the inadequacies of her boss. Credlin was certainly abrasive, and she broke the cardinal rule of political staffers – be neither seen nor heard – but it was extraordinary listening to a minor flotilla of Liberal men transfer the animosity they should have directed at Abbott towards his chief of staff.

Greens Senator Sarah Hanson-Young had to take a male Senate colleague to court to make the point that gratuitous sexist abuse really shouldn't be the workplace norm on the floor of the parliament. Women raised their voices about bullying during the extraordinary week where the right faction of the Liberal Party tried and failed to crunch the numbers for Peter Dutton to take the leadership from Malcolm Turnbull in 2018. During that same period, Australia's former foreign minister and perennial deputy Liberal leader Julie Bishop (characterised by Abbott in 2009 as a 'loyal girl') momentarily forgot her place and ran to be leader of the party, imagining her public popularity and high-level ministerial experience might somehow be an asset. Her own moderate faction spurned her, and she was trampled by blokes who knew better.

As the evidence accumulated, being disconcerted about the sum of these parts escalated to anger and frustration. I was nursing these sensations without realising it; they were present, but recessed. Then, in early 2021, when one of my press gallery colleagues, the news.com.au political editor Samantha Maiden, broke a story, something in my professional consciousness shifted. This was the point where my patience, and the patience of many women in and around politics, ended.

The Gillard prime ministership had taught me sexism in the people's business – politics – wasn't obsolete. The intervening years only reinforced that insight. Then, in early 2021, I learnt something else. Being a woman was actually relevant to documenting these facts, these experiences. I understand this epiphany might sound fatuous. I understand that readers might at this juncture say, well, of course, you bloody idiot. But given the sum of my professional conditioning, given how seriously I took my apprenticeship, given how fundamental those early cues were about detachment being the root of journalistic authority, giving myself permission to report as a woman, as a narrator whose gender furnished some practical insight, was a step change. Not a new way of seeing, but a new way of speaking.

What I understood in early 2021 was that I had the accumulated life experiences of a woman in her early fifties. This wasn't an impediment to my professionalism that needed to be apologised for or anonymised through the studious application of a generic, genderless, formulaic journalistic voice. If I wanted the culture to change, it was actually critically important that I document the story and its aftermath using the voice and sensibility of a professional woman who had observed this subculture and the status-quo-preserving power dynamics minutely for the better part of two decades.

Perhaps this is why Aaron Patrick, a journalist for the *Australian Financial Review*, a person I had worked alongside years before, felt compelled to write a news analysis piece contending that the allegation made public by Maiden (a journalist categorised in the piece as 'spiky' and 'difficult') had created 'a schism through political journalism, exposing a shift in the centre of gravity from the male perspective to the female'. Patrick saw 'Angry coverage that often strayed into unapologetic activism [coming] forth from a new, female media leadership'. I was name-checked among the newly arrived activists, along with other press gallery veterans including Laura Tingle and Karen Middleton.

Given we'd been reporting from Canberra for years, had won awards, managed bureaus, written books and Quarterly Essays, had honorary doctorates conferred on us, it's fair to say we were initially confused by Patrick apparently failing to notice us until early 2021. *Where have all these angry women come from?* had us hooting with laughter. But it was actually a very helpful piece on a number of levels. I suspect what Patrick was really trying to capture was the tonal shift. He was trying to pinpoint something he felt was new.

The innovation was owning our collective life experience in shared space; understanding the universality of the female quest not to be violated, or shamed, or disdained, or talked over, or ignored, and using that as a bridge to reach readers and viewers. Owning these essential truths rather than reporting around them with clinical detachment also changed the rules of engagement between press gallery reporters and the government of the day.

Perhaps Patrick conceptualised our collective reportage during this period as our own versions of the misogyny speech – as if a bunch of news-generating algorithms suddenly assumed human form, put on lipstick and broke the fourth wall.

Patrick wasn't the only male inhabitant of our ecosystem unsettled by the step change. I suspect many of my male colleagues would have preferred to focus on stage-three tax cuts than to linger on what after-hours activity in the parliamentary precinct might reveal about the toxic culture of politics. Scott Morrison and his colleagues also wanted to move past the incident as soon as humanly possible, but the prime minister's tactical ignorance proved to be a radicalising force. It blew the lid right off Parliament House. As Morrison went into political management mode, the fury in the building intensified. Female political staff wept. When they weren't weeping, they raged at the indignity of a workplace and culture that remained institutionally hostile to women almost a decade after Gillard had left the building.

I will not. There was a clear echo of Gillard in the collective show of defiance. The anger spilt out of Parliament House and into the streets as women marched for justice. *Not now, not ever.* Around the building, in my inbox, women were urging persistence. Keep reporting this. We are relying on you. Nothing will change unless you keep pushing. Again, the echo of Gillard skewering Abbott in October 2012, as if the words were etched on the walls of the chambers.

He could change his behaviour, he could apologise for all his past statements and he could apologise for standing next to signs describing me as a witch and a bitch . . . He could change standards himself if he sought to do so. But we will see none of that from the Leader of the Opposition, because on these questions he is incapable of change.

•

Can things change? Can we reach a point in time where a future female occupant of The Lodge won't have to worry about facing the same treatment Gillard faced?

The answer to this question is simple. Things have already changed.

Sometimes change can be hard to see. But, trust me, the progress of the past decade becomes much clearer if you go back and look at what was said about Gillard when she was prime minister; if you recap all the gendered vitriol and then try to imagine a universe where those things would be said, and amplified, now. A culture of impunity has shifted, in increments, to a culture of consequences.

When she left the prime ministership, Gillard predicted things would be easier for the woman who came next. At the time, that prediction felt incredibly optimistic. But I think she's right. Gillard's experiences in the prime ministership raised consciousness in Australia that the equality battle was far from over. The #MeToo movement has also shone light in dark corners, and given women a permission structure to talk about discrimination, harassment and predation.

Obviously, the patriarchy has not been routed. Obviously, progress isn't linear. Progress is generally two steps forward, one step sideways and one back. But women occupying shared public space have become more comfortable about calling out atrocious behaviour. That's what's happened in the decade since Gillard stood at the despatch box and let rip with that speech. Cultural change.

In Gillard's former theatre of politics, there has also been practical change. The events of early 2021 sparked a rare session of introspection among Australia's political class. Politics was compelled to assess its own customs, standards, behaviours, expectations. Prime Minister Morrison commissioned an independent review by Australia's sex discrimination commissioner, Kate Jenkins, which found that one in three staffers interviewed had been sexually harassed while working in Commonwealth parliamentary workplaces. Jenkins recommended significant changes to human resources practices in political offices.

The 2022 federal election result provides another measure of tangible progress. Morrison's inept handling of parliament's own #MeToo moment infuriated many women. In the run-up to the campaign, we saw the birth of a feminised political movement – the so-called 'teal' independents. The 'doctors' wives' of the hoary old political pundits' cliché in Australia had become the doctors, hankering for their own buffer state in our democracy. These independents picked up six seats in the Liberal Party's metropolitan heartland on a platform of gender equality, climate action and integrity in politics – the biggest electoral realignment on the centre-right in Australia since the advent of the Australian Democrats in the 1970s.

After leaving political life, Gillard has continued to enlarge the space for women's leadership. Unlike some of her contemporaries, she has not hovered on the edges of politics, relitigating her legacy. But Gillard did return to the fray for the 2022 campaign – a campaign that seemed to bookend a year where Australian women insisted on being heard. Labor was promising voters cheaper childcare, pay equity and stronger protections against sexual harassment at work.

On 20 May 2022, Gillard stood next to Anthony Albanese in Adelaide. Instead of being intent on filing, as I was back in

October 2012, I permitted myself the luxury of standing up from my desk and wandering to a place in my office where I could watch the press conference. It was incredibly rare to see Gillard engaged on the hustings, so it was obvious she had something to say, and I wanted to listen rather than process the event journalistically.

Gillard spoke to the women who had stopped in their offices at work or looked up from their caring responsibilities a decade earlier to listen when Australia's first female prime minister demanded something better than sexist invective. *I will not.* She launched a call to action: 'if you want to make a better choice, please, tomorrow, go to your ballot places, go to your polling stations and vote Labor and vote for Albo to be prime minister – I am very confident it will be a government for women.'

On 21 May 2022, Morrison was swept from office. On 23 May, Albanese was sworn in as the 31st Prime Minister of Australia.

I don't often watch Question Time, but on that day I happened to have the television on and was half-watching when Julia Gillard rose to speak against a motion moved by opposition leader Tony Abbott. As she spoke, and I began to focus on what she was saying, I gave the screen my full attention. Clearly, something remarkable was happening. It was quite incredible to hear our first woman prime minister say the words, 'I will not be lectured about sexism and misogyny by this man. I will not,' and then proceed to demolish him. Her examples were cogent and on target, painting a vivid and accurate picture of Mr Abbott's contempt for women's equality. But then she got very personal and described her own feelings of being offended at the many ways and occasions that Abbott had attacked her. She put on the record the vile things he had said and done to demean and diminish her, and she left no one who heard or watched the speech in any doubt as to her feelings about having been described as 'a man's bitch' or about it being said that her father had died of shame.

As I listened, I felt a sense of elation that Julia Gillard was fighting back, and doing it so publicly – at the despatch box in the House of Representatives – and with such eloquence. This was a speech for the ages, I felt. No member of parliament, let alone a prime minister, had ever given a speech like this. It was rousing and energising and gave me a sense of the power we feel when we take on those who would seek to keep us downtrodden and impotent. The press gallery reaction to the speech was risible, and very quickly revised. They got it so wrong. Women around the country – and, indeed, around the world – heard a very different speech from the one the journalists ridiculed. They heard a woman leading us all in the fight against sexism and misogyny, and they, like me sitting at home watching her on television, knew that she had done something very profound.

Anne Summers, Australian journalist and author

'What's the worst misogyny you've had to deal with in your career?' Responses from *A Podcast of One's Own*

I was asked to screen test for a history documentary series that the ABC was making about nation-building, and I was eminently qualified for it. I passed my screen test with flying colours. I was told that there was no doubt that I could do the job, but that 'Australia wasn't ready for a female authority figure to tell them their history yet.' And I just about gave up the ghost at that point. You know, it's one of those things. Do you spill the beans? Do you lift the lid? Or do you accept their logic: it's a very small town, a very small industry – 'You'll never work in this town again, girlie!'

So, I didn't say anything at the time, but I got my revenge years later. I convinced the ABC to make a documentary about how Australia was the first country in the world where white women won full political equality: the right to vote and the right to stand for parliament. It was called *Utopia Girls*. I wrote and presented that documentary, and I did eventually get my shot. But it was still making what they considered to be 'a women's story'. So, therefore, it was understandable that you would have a woman fronting it. I would like to think that it wouldn't happen again now, that the people with the power to make those sorts of decisions are less blatantly sexist and more accepting of a woman's authority to tell all of the stories.

Clare Wright, Australian historian, author and broadcaster

Chapter 3

Choirs, TikToks and tea towels: How the misogyny speech travelled around the world

Kathy Lette

It's time for misogynists to be called out on their dirty deeds and to clean up their act. That was the thought on my mind as I washed my hands while chanting my favourite Covid-safe handwashing anthem. 'And in so doing I say to the Leader of the Opposition: I will not be lectured about sexism and misogyny by this man. I will not. And the government will not be lectured about sexism and misogyny by this man. Not now, not ever.'

As I recited, my dangling misogyny speech earrings beat time on my lobes. They're glittery silver and spell out some choice phrases from Julia Gillard's legendary political smackdown.

Back at my computer, I'm now watching two goldfish circle a tank as part of an experimental musical sequence inspired by the infamous oration that wiped the smirk off Tony Abbott's face.

Scrolling through my phone, I find inventive memes inspired by Julia's monologue and cheeky TikTok performances responding to the speech in various ways. There's also a musical minestrone of

Hand-washing technique with soap and water

And in so doing

I say to the

Leader of the Opposition:

I will not be lectured

about sexism and misogyny

by this man.

I will not.

And the government

will not be lectured

about sexism and misogyny

by this man.

Not now,

not ever.

Image generated at washyourlyrics.com. Adapted from the UK National Health Service and the World Health Organization

versions of the misogyny speech, from opera and rap to a cappella and jazz.

This is because Julia's scathing take-down of her political opponent has become part of the pop culture canon. Ballets, theatre pieces, hymns, breakdance routines – people from all over the world, of all ages, have felt inspired to pay homage to the words of Australia's first female prime minister.

There's plenty of wacky merchandise on offer, too – stickers, mugs, phone cases, clothing, posters, tea towels – all celebrating this iconic soliloquy.

When Julia Gillard lined up Tony Abbott in her sights and shot from the lip, each word a bullseye bullet, the women of the world cheered her on. We felt validated, vindicated and victorious as she blew holes in the man's hypocrisy, misogyny and plain ratbag behaviour. In 2020, readers of *The Guardian* voted this blast of feminist fury the 'most unforgettable' moment in Australian TV history, ahead of Gough Whitlam's Dismissal speech, Cathy Freeman's historic gold medal win at the 2000 Olympics, and even Scott and Charlene's wedding on *Neighbours*.[1] The ABC's video of the speech has had more than 3.7 million views online.[2]

Overnight, 'Gillard' became one of the world's top trending words on Twitter, and the speech made headlines in the United States, the United Kingdom, India, South Africa and Canada in the days that followed.[3]

Australian journalist Amelia Lester even suggested in an article for the *New Yorker* that Barack Obama ought to consult the PM for debating lessons: 'supporters of President Obama, watching Gillard cut through the disingenuousness and feigned moral outrage of her opponent to call him out for his own personal prejudice, hypocrisy, and aversion to facts, might be wishing their man would take a lesson from Australia.'[4] What particularly dazzled was Gillard's encapsulation of Abbott's tendency to go for gold in the hypocrisy Olympics: 'if he wants to know what misogyny looks like in modern Australia he does not need a motion in the House of Representatives; he needs a mirror.'

A blog post on the website Jezebel the day after the speech called Julia 'badass', under the headline 'Best thing you'll see all day: Australia's female Prime Minister rips misogynist a new one in epic speech on sexism'.[5]

But even as the speech was sending shock waves around the globe, the myopic, male-dominated Canberra press gallery was writing it off as 'embarrassing', 'blatantly opportunistic' and 'indefensible'.[6] Their dismissive cynicism came as no surprise to Australian women. Even though our country was the first in the world to allow women to stand for parliament, it's always been very blokey Down Under. 'Why do women exist? . . . So men have something to lie down on while having a shag,' runs a typical joke. 'Why don't women surf? . . . It's so hard to get the smell out of the fish.'

As Julia rose to senior roles within the Australian Labor Party, the average Aussie male was quaking in his Ugg boots. Because Julia was not just a 'sheila'; she was a childless, proudly undomesticated agnostic, shacked up with a hairdresser to whom she was not married.

Ms Gillard didn't even have time to strap on her psychological seatbelt in case of a bumpy ride before the roller-coaster began.

The first controversy concerned a 2005 photo shoot at Julia's home in Melbourne. Why was this scandalous? Because in one photo, taken in her kitchen, her fruit bowl was empty. This 'eerily stark', 'chilling'[7] sight was allegedly proof that Gillard was a poor homemaker. Never mind that she had just boomeranged back home from an overseas trip and had not even had time to unpack her suitcase when the photographers arrived. Two years later, in 2007, right-wing senator Bill Heffernan described her as 'deliberately barren', implying that a woman is little more than a life support system for her ovaries, and that to be otherwise made her somehow not fit for political office.

But there was much worse inanity to come. One morning in 2013, in London, where I have lived, on and off, for the past 30 years, I received an urgent message from a producer at the BBC: Would I comment on the latest outrage committed by the Australian prime minister? I quailed. What could it be? Considering the limbo-low bar set by the behaviour of other world leaders, I prepared for the worst. Would it be underage 'bunga bunga' sex parties, à la Berlusconi? An illicit Clinton-style encounter with an intern? The former prime minister of Romania had recently been sentenced to prison for corruption, and the Czech PM was being investigated for misconduct and abuse of power . . . My mind boggled. I rang the producer with trepidation.

'What terrible misdemeanour has Ms Gillard committed?' I inquired.

'Knitting.'

'I'm sorry . . . *Knitting?*'

'Yes. Apparently she's been pictured in *Women's Weekly*, knitting. It's front-page news in Australia.'

Shock! Horror! Men in power can get away with sowing whole plantations of wild oats, yet Julia was being hoisted on her own knitting needle for crafting a cuddly toy.

'And why is that so contentious?' I asked the producer, bemused.

'Because Australian pundits say it's pandering to the female vote.'

I asked the producer if these same pundits were exercised by the fact that 'Iron Man' Abbott constantly pandered to the stereo-typical male macho vote by being photographed performing his Rural Fire Service duties, or surf life saving in budgie smugglers so tight you could detect the man's religion. Apparently, they were not.

This 'news' story turned me into a knitter, too – I was constantly knitting my brows in fury at the treatment meted out to Australia's first female prime minister. I wanted to impale various men on the end of those notorious knitting needles, as so many conservative politicians and shock-jock radio hosts set about proving that dinosaurs still roamed the earth.

At rallies against the government's proposed carbon tax in 2011, opposition leader Tony Abbott was photographed smiling in front of protesters holding placards that read 'Ditch the witch', among other insults. Political cartoonist Larry Pickering depicted our prime minister in a multitude of lewd and derogatory ways, including naked and wearing a strap-on dildo (for which he received a temporary ban from Facebook in June 2012). In August 2012, David Farley, the CEO of one of Australia's largest agriculture companies, commented at a conference about a new machine designed for use in abattoirs that 'It's designed for non-productive old cows – Julia Gillard's got to watch out.'

At this point, members of the British media started to ask me whether Australia was being overrun by a plethora of political pterodactyls, or some other equally antiquated species such as real-life Sir Les Pattersons. And it was hard to disagree. Over the course of Gillard's prime ministership, the bullying and gendered attacks intensified. In 2013, instead of interviewing the PM about government policy, one Perth radio host badgered her about the sexuality of her 'hairdresser' boyfriend.[8] The implication was that if the First Bloke was gay, then clearly Julia might also play for the other team. Julia was calm and courteous throughout, while every woman listening wanted to beat the interviewer to a pulp with her curling tongs.

This relentless sexism reached its peak in 'Menugate'. The misogyny du jour on the in-house menu at a Liberal Party fund-raising dinner in March 2013 was named 'Julia Gillard Kentucky Fried Quail', which featured 'Small Breasts, Huge Thighs' served in a 'Big Red Box'.

There was a collective cringe of revulsion and shocked disbelief from the women of Australia. We thought back to Julia's misogyny speech, when she did not just lie back and think of Canberra but rather served up her own dish on the parliamentary menu – male chauvinist pig on a spit, skewering her smirking nemesis and leaving him squirming. In Britain, France and the United States, Julia's impromptu tongue-lashing was praised as the most out-spoken attack on sexism in political history – and yet, clearly, nothing in Australia had changed.

Although the *Sydney Morning Herald* registered a 5 per cent jump in Julia's approval rating after the furore caused by the misogyny speech, much of the mainstream Australian media continued to write off the speech as a disaster. Political journalist Lenore Taylor, then working for the *Sydney Morning Herald*, put this down to the male dominance of news journalism.[9]

An analysis of British national newspapers around the time of the misogyny speech by the UK organisation Women in Journalism revealed that sexist, humiliating stereotypes of women and male by-lines dominated the front pages; during one month alone, male journalists wrote 78 per cent of all front-page articles, and men accounted for 84 per cent of the people mentioned or quoted in lead stories. When powerful women were featured, the images were mostly unflattering and un-businesslike. All the fellas featured, however, looked put-together in suits or sports gear. Men were invariably portrayed as active participants in life, while women were predominantly presented as sexualised objects.[10] But even these often-sexist journals reported Julia's speech as a success. Only the Australian papers declined to do so.

My European pals often ask me to explain the antipathy to women in the Antipodes. I joke that it dates back to 1788, when Australia was basically colonised by boatloads of blokes and sheep – which is why the Aussie version of foreplay is shearing. ('Why are there women? . . . Because sheep can't type,' runs another sexist 'joke' I just remembered.) But whatever the reason, is it any wonder Australian women are starting to wonder whether it's time to take the 'men' out of Mensa?

If we are talking about conservative politicians, the answer's clearly yes. Over the past few decades, misogynistic misdemeanours have been piling up on each other like circus acrobats. In March 2021, some of these events prompted the March 4 Justice, with hundreds of thousands of people protesting around the nation for justice, accountability and women's safety.

Later in the same year, videos emerged of male government advisers engaging in sexual activity within the parliament buildings. In footage leaked to the media (an unfortunate term under the circumstances) one man is seen masturbating and then ejaculating onto a female MP's desk;[11] giving new meaning to the term 'desk job'.

Allegations of sexual misconduct then escalated when media commentator Peta Credlin, who was chief of staff to Tony Abbott while he was PM, claimed that a group of government staff members had held regular orgies in the middle of the day while MPs were in parliament for Question Time.[12] (It's not known if orgy participants wrote letters of appreciation on parliamentary note paper – 'Thank you for coming . . .')

It's also been alleged that the prayer and meditation room in Parliament House is regularly used as a quickie venue for many busy parliamentary employees keen on a different kind of religious experience – well, they do call out 'Oh God! Oh God!' quite a lot. Although, being egotistical male pollies, at the peak point of satisfaction I suspect they're more likely to call out their own names.

And what was then Prime Minister Scott Morrison's response to this litany of dirty deeds? When the backlash sent his conservative government sliding in the polls, 'Scotty from Marketing' retaliated with a toe-curlingly mawkish press conference in which he blubbed about how much he loved his wife, mum and daughters. It was a real two-hanky job – but was also a little like trying to put out a bushfire with a damp squeegee.

It should be said, however, that Aussie politicians falling on their pork swords is nothing new. And, sadly, sexism is prevalent on both sides of politics. In 2008, New South Wales Labor Party MP Matt Brown was appointed Minister for Police and invited some intimate friends back to his office to celebrate. The celebration featured the minister stripping to his jocks, leaping on his sofa and, there's no polite way of putting this, offering to 'titf*ck' the nearest woman. He still holds the record for the briefest stint as police minister – four days.

In 1995, Martin Ferguson, then president of the Australian Council of Trade Unions (and later Labor politician) described women campaigning for paid maternity leave as 'hairy-legged femocrats'. One-time Labor Party leader Mark Latham whinged in 2006 that 'Australian mates and good blokes have been replaced by nervous wrecks, metrosexual knobs and toss-bags' thanks to 'the rise of Left-feminism in the 1970s and 1980s, with its sanitising impact on public culture'.[13]

Some male pundits willingly excuse this behaviour as jokey, matey banter and laddish bonhomie. They deride women for not being able to 'take a joke'. So, perhaps the answer is to fight back on their 'hilarious' terms. Next time a man tells a sexist joke to embarrass or unnerve the women in the room, why not simply ask him if he knows why 'dumb blonde' jokes are always one-liners? . . . So that men can understand them. Or maybe try asking him if he knows the difference between government bonds and blokes? . . . Government bonds mature. If a David Farley type should ever refer to you as a 'cow' or a 'silly moo', just point out sweetly that the reason men can't get mad cow disease is because they're pigs. And if he retorts that women can't tell jokes, just reply: 'That's because we vote for them, thanks to the under-representation of women in politics.'

Of course, the sexual morals of British politicians are beyond reproach . . . it's been *months* since Boris Johnson got a new woman pregnant. In 2020, then Prime Minister Johnson was forced to defend Tony Abbott's appointment as an adviser to the UK government on international trade.[14] Perhaps the two ex-PMs can now get together to discuss Johnson's views on the ways to deal with a female colleague – that is, 'Just pat her on the bottom and send her on her way', as Johnson wrote in 2005.[15] Or they could brainstorm about what to do with the children of single mothers, who are 'ill-raised, ignorant, aggressive and illegitimate' – another enlightened view expressed by the former UK prime minister.[16] Tory MP Neil Parish's tractor porn, Chris Pincher's sexual misconduct, the convictions of sex offenders Imran Ahmad Khan and Charlie Elphicke – the list of British Conservative political sexual scandals goes on and on. So, it's important to remember that sexism thrives in both hemispheres.

The only cure is to get more women into government. And Julia Gillard's fabled attack on misogyny is the feminist rocket fuel we need to do just that.

When Prime Minister Gillard left office, she delivered her parting comments with dignity and courage – 'It'll be easier for the next woman,' she said, while young women who were present in the room wept openly. Nearly a decade later, it's high time these same women told their male colleagues that they no longer want his seat on the bus; they want his seat in parliament.

That will be Julia's true and lasting legacy. Because, unlike Margaret Thatcher, the United Kingdom's first woman prime minister, Julia Gillard did not pull up the career ladder behind her. Australia's first female prime minister has obviously not only been wearing a bulletproof bra all these years, but she's also proved that women are each other's human Wonderbras – uplifting, support-ive and making each other look bigger and better – exemplified by her work with the Global Institute for Women's Leadership and the Campaign for Female Education.

And young women are responding to Julia's invitation to work towards leadership positions. This is in part attributable to the social media platform TikTok, which is ticking all the right boxes by bringing Julia's misogyny speech to vast new audiences around the world. In 2020, Melbourne-based recording artist and TikTok queen Abbey Hansen (known on the platform as @minorfauna) mashed up the speech with Doja Cat's 'Boss Bitch'. This went viral, with more than 1.6 million views and with more than one thousand videos that have since used the edited audio.[17] There are even TikTok videos of women getting tattoos that read *Not Now, Not Ever*.

If you want to join the chorus of appreciation celebrating the ten-year anniversary of Julia's iconic speech, but you feel a tattoo is going a tad too far, then why not simply sing along to one of the many adaptations of her blistering oration? There's 'Julia Gillard's Misogyny Speech' by SCABZ (1.2k views on YouTube, 8.7k listens).[18] Or 'The Bad Thing', adapted and performed by Bronwyn Calcutt and friends (52k views on YouTube).[19] If you're more classically inclined, there's the 'Not Now, Not Ever!' choir song, composed by Rob Davidson, performed by the Australian Voices choir (342k views on YouTube).[20]

Or, you could tune in to the recording of 'After Julia', a special concert reflecting on Julia Gillard's prime ministership, which was broadcast live on ABC Classic FM's *New Music Up Late* in 2014. The event featured eight contemporary works by Australian women composers, one of which included the experimental sung interpretation of the movements of the two live goldfish I mentioned earlier.[21]

Alternatively, you could try one of the dance performances on offer, either 'I Was Offended' (Julia Gillard Misogyny Speech Scene) from the work *Mighty* by Lingua Franca Dance Theatre, performed by Kate Smith,[22] or 'JULIA' – a powerful solo dance theatre work by one of Australia's leading contemporary dancers, Natalie Allen.[23]

Or you might visit the National Gallery of Victoria to see the beautiful aquamarine stringybark painting titled *Order*, a radical piece of Indigenous art by Dhambit Munungurr, a prolific Yolŋu artist who works in the north-east Arnhem Land community of Yirrkala. In the painting, sheepish and ashamed male politicians cower in the shadow of a gigantic Julia. She is fierce and fabulous, and surrounded by Yolŋu dancers who are dancing, embodying a Yolŋu songline and leaping in as her bodyguards.[24]

Finally, you could also call out misogyny and sexism by joining in the next time thousands of Australian women march in rallies demanding more robust responses to sexual harassment and assault, and an end to 'rape culture', as they did in 2021.[25]

And if you are going on a march, you might as well put your best foot forward wearing misogyny speech memorabilia. My custom-made 'Not Now, Not Ever' bovver boots constantly remind me to kick misogyny to the kerb. Just as my friend, the formidable and fabulous Ms Julia Gillard, did on the day when she stood at the despatch box and pronounced, loud and clear, 'I will not be lectured about sexism and misogyny by this man. I will not.'

2020 landed my sister and me in two weeks quarantine, where I made TikToks to entertain us.

Disheartened by our leader in a time of crisis, I thought back to 2012. Walking into uni, finding everyone huddled around a screen. It was the misogyny speech.

After three takes, I'd reimagined the speech that instilled me with courage and urged me to take more notice of politics as a young woman.

I'd hoped to entertain my sister, but ended up going viral with the positive impact Julia's speech had on me. Including standing up to the raw-onion-eating misogynists of the world.

Abbey Hansen, Australian musician and creator of the viral misogyny speech/'Boss Bitch' TikTok

'What's the worst misogyny you've had to face?' Responses from *A Podcast of One's Own*

Witnessing what happened to Julia Gillard as prime minister was a reminder of how deeply entrenched misogyny is, and it was demoralising because you realised that you could ascend to literally the highest office in the land and people would still treat you as if you didn't deserve to be there. If I argued about how sexist people were, people would respond, 'Well, everyone in power gets it, people made fun of John Howard's eyebrows,' as if there is any equivalency between that and the things cartoonists got away with drawing about Julia Gillard. It's not any single example, but it's realising that there is a language of misogyny that is so innate to so many people – that is their primary language, almost – sometimes, on your less optimistic days, it feels like you are trying to push a big barrel of shit up a mountain and it's almost inconceivable that you could get to the top.

Clementine Ford, Australian writer and speaker

Part Two

MISOGYNY PAST AND PRESENT

Chapter 4

The history and culture of misogyny, from the ancient world to today

Mary Beard

More than two thousand years ago, sometime in the seventh century BCE, a poet and songster on the Greek island of Amorgos composed verses to be sung at an all-male drinking party (all-male, that is, apart from the enslaved women and girls who were there for the 'use' of the men). The poet, Semonides, entertained the audience with a song about the 'females of the species', and in particular about the wives whom the guests had left back at home.

He went through the different varieties of wife a man might have, comparing each one to an animal: the 'pig wife', who lives in a house of filth; the 'weasel wife', sex-crazed and thieving; the ugly 'monkey wife', who looks hideous and is a laughing stock throughout town ('she's got no neck . . . / no butt, spindly legs. / Pity the poor man / who holds such a ghastly creature in his arms'). There was just a single specimen who was actually desirable. That was the 'bee wife', 'the only one on whom no blame settles . . . she grows / old having borne handsome and illustrious children . . . /

She doesn't enjoy sitting with the other women when they are talking sex.[1]

It is all too easy to imagine the tipsy men of Amorgos enjoying this entertainment in the classic traditions of ancient Greek misogyny. Most women, Semonides insists, are as much animal as they are human (listen to how they yap, snarl and grunt). Depending on exactly which breed a man has ended up with, his wife will be lazy or liable to eat her husband out of house and home, will have sex with anyone, will be an ugly trickster or a vain, deceptive seducer, two-faced and dangerous. In some lines that are extreme even by ancient Greek standards – and which have driven some more sensitive (or timid) modern university departments to remove the full version of the poem from their curriculum – Semonides observes that there are some wives you can't shut up, even if 'in anger you take a stone and knock their / teeth out'.

That threat of violence is an important reminder that misogyny occupies a spectrum which goes from everyday sexism, through entrenched prejudice to murderous hate-crime, or femicide. How the different parts of that spectrum are distinguished or connected has always been hard to pin down. It would obviously be naive to think that there was some direct progression from the sexual banter of the male drinking party to brutal violence against women. We should not imagine that the men of Amorgos necessarily went home at the end of the evening to beat up their wives. But it would be equally naive to imagine that there was no connection at all. At the very least, the 'joke' (as I am sure they would have called it, and as some scholars still do) about knocking out teeth would have served to normalise violence, to provide a context in which that could seem a legitimate action or response. In much the same way, the ancient caricature of women as a wasteful drain on men's resources no doubt underpinned the practice, which is documented in some parts of the Greco-Roman world, of selectively killing baby girls at birth. The caricature certainly did not *cause* female infanticide, but it was one of the cultural factors which normalised it.

My own concerns in this chapter are not with trying to pin down those tricky connections, though such issues are bound to hover in the background. I want instead to explore some of the ways that misogyny has appeared in art and literature, from the ancient world right up to today, and in different cultural traditions. Even though my focus is more on the past than the present, I want to reflect on how those historical traditions of misogyny can be challenged or subverted *now*. I have no interest in removing most of the offending texts and images from public view, from the bookstore and library, or from the educational curriculum. If misogyny, broadly defined, were to be a touchstone for permanent exclusion, there would be little left in some major art galleries – and we would be losing a lot if we decided to censor sections of Homer's *Odyssey*, or Shakespeare, or Mozart's operas on similar grounds. My interest is quite the reverse, in fact. If our history is a history of misogyny, what do we do about that? I think it is only by looking the culture of misogyny in the eye that we can stand up to it, put it in its place, understand what drives it and hopefully do better.

This is exactly what British artist Sonia Boyce tried to do, using rather different tactics, when – as part of a series of 'performances' in Manchester Art Gallery in 2018 – she provocatively removed from the walls J. W. Waterhouse's painting *Hylas and the Nymphs* (1896). Based on a Greek myth, this shows seven pubescent, naked water nymphs enticing the innocent young Hylas into their pool, from which – drowned or ensnared by the women – he will never return. The provocation worked and the removal caused an outcry: killjoy feminists, it was claimed, had taken down a much-loved painting. ('Feminism gone mad!' was one succinct, and predictable, comment.) But it was a tease. Boyce's point was that the removal was only ever meant to be a temporary intervention, and was intended to prompt those who loved the painting, or simply took it for granted, to look harder and think about what it actually depicted: sexually predatory girls (and they are no older than that) enticing a man to his death; voracious females trapping their male victim.

In the Western tradition, misogyny has been hardwired into culture from ancient times onwards, which is one of the reasons it has proved so hard to get rid of. Some of the classical examples, such as Semonides' poetic rant, are glaringly obvious. To take another, in Euripides' play *Hippolytus*, which was first performed in Athens in 428 BCE, there is one moment in particular that has always been in the misogyny top ten. The young prince Hippolytus has vowed himself to chastity and the worship of the virgin goddess Artemis – and at one point in the play he utters this misogynist's charter, addressing Zeus, the king of the gods:

O Zeus, why have you created women to live in the light of the sun, a deceitful evil for mankind? If you wanted to prop-agate the human race, you should not have done this through women. Rather men should deposit bronze or iron or heavy gold in your temples as a purchase price for any offspring. They should buy their children . . . and they should live in their houses free from women. It is clear that woman is a great evil – after all, in order to get rid of the evil, the father who gave her life and brought her up attaches a dowry to her when he sends her away from home. And then the man who takes this pernicious creature into his house rejoices as he tricks out his disastrous idol with lovely jewels and decks her in robes to perfection, poor man, as he gradually drains his house of its wealth. Things are easiest for the man whose wife is a nothing. Even so, it is harmful to have a woman set up in all her silliness in one's home. Yet it is the clever woman that I detest. May I never have in my house a woman who is more intelligent than a woman should be.[2]

There is something immediately chilling when you imagine the audience at the Athenian theatre (again, very likely an all-male audience) listening to this. And there is something horribly unsurprising about the way the figure of Hippolytus has been adopted by modern 'Red Pill' online communities: disaffected and discontented men who are united in their resentment of women (as well as of people of colour and 'the left'). Hippolytus is an especially potent symbol for their 'cause', because the plot of Euripides' play hinges on a false rape allegation against Hippolytus – such allegations being seen by many in the 'Red Pill' misogynist world as a powerful weapon, used by dangerous and deceitful women to destroy the lives of innocent men.

Looking back, however, over my fifty or so years of studying ancient cultures, I am surprised at how much of this misogyny I missed for so long. Sometimes, that was because it was literally 'translated away'. When I was a student, we rarely referred, for example, to all the *rapes* that feature throughout Ovid's famous multi-volume poem the *Metamorphoses* – the rape of Europa by Jupiter, in the form of a bull, the rape of Danae by Jupiter, again, this time in the form of a shower of gold, and dozens more drawn from the repertoire of ancient mythology. We talked instead about '*ravishings*', as if the act was, if not consensual, then at least welcome – as well as vaguely religious. It is perhaps a similar spin that allows the image of the rape of Europa to appear, apparently unproblematically, on the Greek 2-euro coin. Few people seem to bridle at what is a scene of sexual assault jangling around on the coins in their pocket.

More often, I missed the misogyny because, somehow, I just took it for granted, and did not really register what was on the page or in front of my eyes. I must have been reading Homer's *Odyssey* for well over thirty years before I realised that, at the very start of the poem (and close to the very beginnings of the traditions of Western literature), we read of the silencing of women, the straightforward denial of a woman's right to a voice. The lines in question feature Penelope, who has been waiting for years for her husband, Odysseus, to return from the Trojan War to their home on the island of Ithaca – all the while resisting demands by her 'suitors' that she should give him up for dead and marry one of them. (Her trick has been to say that she would consider remarrying only when she had finished weaving the burial shroud for her elderly father-in-law, but to unpick her work each evening, so that she never finishes.) Homer explains how on one occasion the canny Penelope came downstairs from her room to find a bard singing songs of the disasters facing Odysseus and the other Greeks as they made their way home. Not unreasonably, she asked him to sing something a little less upsetting. At that point her still wet-behind-the-ears teenaged son, Telemachus, intervened and, after telling her not to blame the bard, said: 'Mother, go back up into your quarters and take up your own work, the loom and the distaff . . . speech will be the business of men, all men, and of me most of all, for mine is the power in this household.'[3] And off she went. It is a foundational moment in Western literature: the first time that a son is caught telling his mum to shut up (in fact, more precisely, the first time that a son proves his manhood *by* telling his mum to shut up: this is a coming-of-age moment for young Telemachus). Over years of close reading, I am ashamed to say I had simply not noticed.

Nor for a long time did I see the point of the images of Amazon women that were so common in ancient Greek art. These Amazons were a mythical race of female warriors, who supposedly lived on the margins of the 'civilised' Greek world – and were so committed to their women-only society that they used men just temporarily, for procreation, and put to death (or sent back to their fathers) any baby boys who were born. Said to be the implacable enemies of the Greeks, they were pictured *everywhere*, from painted vases to the sculptures of the Parthenon, fighting against male Greek warriors. I suppose I used to take the whole story and its representations as just one more example of the curiosities of Greek myth. But the curiosities of Greek myth always *mean* something. In this case, it is that the women never win. In countless images, in their homes, in cities and temples, Greek men and women saw the transgressive Amazons – women who, in the cultural imagination, broke through the conventions of proper female behaviour – being *killed*. They were as much the enemies of 'civilisation' as were the violent and monstrous, half-man, half-horse centaurs, alongside whom they were prominently displayed on the Parthenon (women and animals, as in Semonides' poem, going together). The basic message was that the only *good* Amazon was a *dead* Amazon.

My own blindness here is instructive. Rather like the gallery-goers whom Sonia Boyce prompted to look harder at Waterhouse's painting, I am afraid I tended to take these cultural symbols for granted; or, at least, they were so ubiquitous that they ceased to be noticeable. The truth is that many of us only *register* the misogyny of the culture we have inherited when we have a reason to look for it. (I think that I only saw the full significance of the silencing of Penelope in the *Odyssey* when I came to write a lecture – later published in my book *Women and Power*[4] – specifically on the female voice in the public sphere.) Or, on other occasions, we spot it when it goes too far even for misogyny's familiar conventions.

That was the case with some of the memorabilia of Donald Trump's US presidential election campaign in 2016. Women in power, from Dilma Rousseff of Brazil to Theresa May of the United Kingdom (and including Julia Gillard herself), have long been caricatured as the gorgon Medusa of Greek mythology. Medusa was a dangerous character with snakes for her hair, who was decapitated by the 'hero' Perseus and then became his most deadly weapon – for her head had the power to turn to stone anyone who looked at it. She appears time and again in 'masterpieces' of Western art as an agent of destruction, or quite literally of *petrification*. And we find her almost as often as a caricature or parody – given the facial features, under those snaky locks, of whatever female politician is the target, and intended to convey the danger and perceived repulsiveness of any powerful woman. But it was only when supporters of Trump started decorating tote bags and coffee mugs with images of the would-be president in the guise of Perseus, brandishing the snaky-locked and oozing severed head of Hillary Clinton, that the murderous violence of the stereotype became clear to many people. There was no pressure, so far as I know, to ban or censor these images, sadistic as they were (in part perhaps because the ensemble was based on – and gained legitimation from – a famous Renaissance statue in Florence of Perseus and Medusa, by Benvenuto Cellini). But it was striking that when the comedian Kathy Griffin reversed the image, and was photographed holding up a gory mask of Donald Trump as if it was his bleeding severed head, she lost her job and was investigated by the US Secret Service. Women, in other words, cannot be seen doing to men what men can be seen doing to women.

In drawing my examples from the Greco-Roman world and its later inheritance, I have been focusing on what I know best. But I certainly do not mean to give the impression that the Greeks and Romans had a monopoly on cultural misogyny. Across the world, different traditions have produced very different art and myth, while telling very similar basic stories – whether that's the figure of Eve in the Judaeo-Christian tradition (associating the creation of woman with the origin of misery for man, much as the creation of the first woman Pandora signalled the origin of toil, hardship and pain for the ancient Greek man); or the Kusozu paintings in Buddhist Japan, which served to remind the faithful not just of the transitory nature of human flesh in general, but also how disgusting women's bodies in particular were (they depict, in a series of images, the gradually decaying, seeping and putrefying corpse of a beautiful girl, making the messy, dirty women of Semonides seem fairly spruce and tame). Every culture that I have ever explored, even briefly, contributes something, somehow, to the repertoire of misogyny.

That is not to say that no powerful women ever appear in art, myth and traditional literature, let alone in 'real life', now or in the past. Of course they do. In addition to the occasional ruler (Elizabeth I of England is one who comes to mind, even though she herself is supposed to have pointed to her 'heart and stomach of a *king*'), religions across the globe have generated divine figures that embody feminine power – albeit often at a cost. The Virgin Mary has power through being what most women are *not*: a virgin. Some goddesses *do* hold sway, though often their symbols of power are actually gendered as male (helmets, spears and shields), and the boundary between the divine and the demonic is a fuzzy one (is a witch powerful or pernicious?).

The point is that the world's museums, art galleries and libraries are full of the long history of misogyny, in word and image – so much 'part of the wallpaper' that even committed feminists sometimes have to be nudged to notice it. What we see around us so frequently falls somewhere along that broad spectrum between everyday sexism and violence against women's bodies that it can seem as if misogyny has traditionally been the default position of world culture. Put simply, art and literature are full of women being put down, dismembered, blamed, praised for knowing their (subservient) place, silenced and raped.

My question is, how far can we challenge that image? Can we see through the cultural misogyny? Can we subvert it? Can we find its weak spots?

One challenge has rested in deep history, and in the idea that – in myth, at least – it is possible to see through the dominant misogyny of the past few thousand years to a very different world where women *did* once hold power, in some primitive matriarchy, but were then overthrown by the rule of men. The Amazons might be faint traces of that matriarchy. So too might be a few images of powerful women who play memorable roles in Greek mythology, such as Queen Clytemnestra, who was said to have ruled in Mycenae while her husband, Agamemnon, was away fighting in the Trojan War (in a very different model of 'what was going on back home while the men were absent' from Odysseus and Penelope's Ithaca).

I have never been sure that an early matriarchy is a particularly comforting notion. If women were once in charge, it is hardly much reassurance to know that they were so comprehensively brought down; nor is it particularly useful to imagine power in such binary gendered terms (*either* rule by men, *or* by women). More important, though – even if no one can now actually be certain of the power relations among our most distant, prehistoric ancestors – is that the logic of this mythology works against any idea that we are glimpsing a few faint vestiges of pre-patriarchal women's power. For the rhetoric of misogyny, and the way it claims to represent the truth about how the world is and should be, does not simply rest on the image of abject, oozing and violated women. One of misogyny's pseudo-justifications for itself is that women have been *shown* to be unfit to rule. That is one of the reasons why the Amazons always lose – you can allow women to be warriors, if you must, but they cannot ever win. And the crucial point about those other powerful women we occasionally glimpse in classical myth is that they always *mis*-use power, mess up and fail.

It is true, for example, that Clytemnestra took control in Mycenae in Agamemnon's absence, but how did she behave? She dominated a weak male lover (who played the 'woman' to her 'man'), and when Agamemnon eventually returned, she murdered him in his bath, and was in turn murdered by her own children, in a cycle of slaughter and vengeance. The bottom line here is that the myth of matriarchy – far from being the remnant of an earlier social and political order – is an argument in favour of the patriarchal status quo. The message is that men *must* rule, because women make a (bloody) mess of it.

Rather than fantasise about prehistory, we should probably accept that misogyny has been the default position throughout all the history to which we have reliable access. If we want to challenge it, we would do better – in part, at least – to work *within* the cultural forms that support it, subverting it from the inside, exposing its inconsistencies, its skewed vision and the anxieties and ambivalences it tries hard to obscure. That is precisely what is being done in a number of very popular modern works of fiction that switch the ancient mythical viewpoint from female to male. Madeline Miller's novel *Circe*, for example, gives Circe – the seductive witch who ensnared Odysseus on his way home from Troy, while turning his companions into pigs – her own story, character, personhood and voice. Almost twenty years ago, Margaret Atwood turned the tables on Odysseus in a similar way. In *The Penelopiad*, she narrated the events at Ithaca from Penelope's point of view, and memorably gave a role to twelve women slaves who were killed by Telemachus in punishment for colluding (and sleeping) with the suitors in the palace. These books adeptly reveal the misogyny that I took so long to notice. But even more important, they show how the patriarchal cultural certainties embedded in these traditional tales can be dramatically destabilised by as simple a tactic as changing the point of view. Misogyny, in part, depends on whose story we are allowed to hear.

The same simple and pointed challenges can be found in modern visual arts, too. One of the most dramatic interventions here is by the American artist Kiki Smith, in a sculpture called *Lilith*. Lilith was a demonic figure in Jewish culture, supposed to be the first wife of Adam and Satan's partner, a malevolent force who attacks babies and refuses to stick to a subservient role. (According to one vivid detail in her tale, she would not lie underneath Adam when they had sex, as it implied that they were not equal.) She is a classic example of the mythical woman whose refusal to play by the rules means danger to the community, and she became a favourite with Western artists from the mid-nineteenth century, often depicted as a sexually transgressive femme fatale.

Smith's 1995 sculpture does something quite different. Her Lilith is a naked figure in bronze, still with enough demonic power to be able to cling upside down to the gallery wall (or so the clever hanging suggests), and with gleaming blue eyes that stare at the viewer. But there is no voyeurism here, no femme fatale (we only clearly see her naked back; her breasts are more or less out of sight) and, crucially, the whole piece was cast from the body of a *real woman*. It is as if to say, 'This is the power of you and me, not of some mythical demon.' Even more surprising, perhaps, is the fact that at least one modern Japanese artist, Fuyuko Matsui, has re-engaged with the traditions of Kusozu and the decaying corpses of women from a female perspective. In an unsettling way, to be sure, her paintings aim to expose the misogyny of the genre, while also recapturing some power for the female body: Matsui's corpses are *self*-mutilating, not passively decaying, and they look directly at the painting's viewer, as if refusing to be the submissive object of a male gaze.

The success of these reappropriations in literature and art are, for me, a hint that the culture of misogyny might be more fragile than it appears. Certainly, misogyny has always made a lot of cultural noise across the world. But it is worth remembering that the most flagrant injustices and inequities, from racism to sexism and beyond, are those that have to shout the loudest in their own defence. One of the purposes of 'culture', after all, is to make seem 'natural' claims that are *not* natural at all; the flimsier the argument, the more noisily it is supported. Once we learn to look misogyny in the eye, we may well also see just how vulnerable it is as an ideology.

That is not seriously to suggest that misogyny can easily be dislodged, or is on its way out any time soon. I have no doubt that it will long survive me. It *is* to say that we could all be more alert to the anxieties and uncertainties that its insistent noise tries to drown out. Indeed, some of these are visible even (or perhaps especially) in the most flagrant examples from ancient Greek culture with which I started. I referred to the chilling picture of the all-male audience at the Athenian theatre listening hard to Hippolytus' rant about the evil of women – and so they might have done. But it is not very likely that they would have been actively cheering him on. Or, if they did, they could not have been giving Euripides' play sufficient attention. For the point of the impossibly extreme version of woman-hating that spewed out of Hippolytus' mouth was to show that it was precisely that: impossibly and destructively extreme. In the play as a whole, Euripides is actually questioning the hardline version of sexual purity and abstinence that Hippolytus represents (while acknowledging that he was the victim of the rape allegation, which leads, when it is believed, to his horrible death). 'Red Pill' communities may be able selectively to extract some slogans from *Hippolytus* that chime with their own prejudices. But its overall message was not at all what they like to think.

So, what about the men from Amorgos enjoying Semonides' nasty after-dinner song about the disgusting, wasteful, voracious and literally *beastly* races of women? They cannot be let off quite so lightly as the Athenians in the theatre. There were no complex and competing moralities here, and we have to imagine an atmosphere somewhere between laddish, drunken revelry and the worst 'locker room'. We still have to ask: who was the 'joke' of the song *on*? It was on the women, and the wives back home, obviously. Yet there might well have been a few at the party who were just about sober enough to see that the joke was on the men too, and on male self-delusions. Scratch the surface, and part of Semonides' point, surely, is that every man in town flatters himself that *he* is married to a virtuous bee woman – when, actually, it stands to reason that *most* of them are hitched to dogs, monkeys and the rest of the animal types. The song, in other words, exposes their misplaced, self-serving self-satisfaction, and it makes a mockery of everyone.

And that – thanks to the seventh century BCE's Semonides – is one of the biggest lessons of the culture of misogyny. It undermines us all, even the men who think it speaks for them.

I can no longer remember where exactly I was when I heard the misogyny speech, just as I can no longer remember a time before it was delivered.

It was a Pandora's box moment, a moment where Cassandra finally had her wise and noble prophecies heard and understood.

It was a moment of profound relief personally and collectively. Julia Gillard spoke to all that we, as women, had been sitting on, all that we had been expected to tolerate. I don't think any of us truly realised until that moment just how heavy, unwieldy and denigrating that burden had been. I wept tears of rage for the years of silence. But I also wept with gratitude for this glimpse of a new horizon made possible by Julia Gillard's moment of great leadership . . . a moment where one person stood up, brimming with soulful experience, devoid of self-interest and spoke for the many.

I believe that none of what we have seen since with the Me Too movement and Time's Up could have happened as fully without this moment courageously seized by Prime Minister Gillard.

Of course, there has been a backlash, but that backlash is not nearly as powerful or meaningful as the seismic awakening Julia Gillard's words evoked in women around the globe about who we are, what we are capable of and how we as women can lead the way to a more respectful and inclusive future.

Cate Blanchett, Australian actor and producer

'What's the worst misogyny you've had to deal with in your career?' Responses from *A Podcast of One's Own*

Some years ago, I had just got my own BBC Radio 4 show. I didn't have an agent and I needed an agent to do the deal, and I thought, what a great time to get a really good agent, because probably only half a dozen people a year get their own Radio 4 show with their name in the title. So, I wrote to all these different agents saying, 'I'm doing this live show, which is being turned into a radio show, and it's already been commissioned.' I was thinking, I'm bringing them 10 per cent of *something* already, there's obviously something to work with. And I got so many emails like this one – 'I'm sorry, I can't take on anyone of the female persuasion. That might sound sexist, but it's not me that's sexist, it's the industry. The industry will only take on a certain amount of women, and we already have enough women on our books.' Another one said, 'We're a bit saturated girl-wise at the moment.' SATURATED. GIRL-WISE! And I actually wrote back and said, 'What does saturation look like for you? What's your gender balance? Because I'm really interested to know what satura-tion looks like.' They didn't respond to that. Someone more senior at the company wrote another email saying, 'We really wish you well!', probably thinking, 'Please don't screenshot those other emails.'

I still have those emails, and I sometimes do look at them. And yes, of course it was a woman who wrote that the industry was sexist! The men didn't bother to write back at all.

Deborah Frances-White, comedian,
author and host of The Guilty Feminist *podcast*

Chapter 5

Misogyny and intersectionality

Aleida Mendes Borges

On a given day, I was strolling along the famous Copacabana waterfront in Rio de Janeiro, Brazil, when I was stopped by a man who asked: 'Do you want to come to my hotel room?'

I was slightly shocked that a stranger would approach me with such a proposition. Not wanting to make a fuss, I politely declined and kept walking. The man was visibly outraged that I would not take him up on his offer and proceeded to ask: 'Is that not what all of you Brazilian women want? To sleep with white tourists from Europe?'

At this point I considered whether to give him a lecture on everything that was wrong with what he had just said, but instead opted to save my energy and swiftly replied that I was not Brazilian. What followed was even more striking as the man transformed into a completely different person, apologising for his behaviour and saying that he should not have asked that. *He thought I was Brazilian.*

My experience of often being mistaken for a Black Brazilian woman throughout Latin America was eye-opening in the sense that it gave me a perspective on how different factors intersect to shape how women are treated. It revealed to me the profound and unique circumstance of being a Black woman in the Americas, as it embodied a complex history of slavery and the consequent legal ownership of Black bodies.

I was born in Cabo Verde, grew up in Portugal and became an adult in the United Kingdom. So, I have been an immigrant for my whole life. I also studied for two years in France and have had the wonderful opportunity to travel, mostly on my own, to more than one hundred countries worldwide. This has meant that although my personal experiences as a Black woman were shaped by a very European context, I have had countless direct experiences of being a Black woman in different societies throughout the Americas, Africa, Europe and Asia.

As asserted by Black feminist scholars since the 1980s, racialised notions of sexuality and gender were not by-products of slavery and colonialism, but foundational to them. White women were held in contrast with those from 'otherised' groups in the context of colonialism to distinguish between the 'marriageable' and the 'sexualised' women. Although both were oppressed subjects, for centuries colonialism meant that non-white women were, and continue to be, both defined *by* their sexuality and *as* their sexuality.[1]

The particularities of almost four hundred years of the trafficking of Black bodies to the Americas meant that they were owned, used and abused as 'breeding machines'. The archipelago of Cabo Verde became strategically important for the Portuguese as a slave market. From the 1460s onwards, young men and women from

West Africa were transported to Cidade Velha, the first European settlement established in the tropics, to be sold and shipped as 'cargo' to the Americas. Slave traders did not travel with their white wives, and so Black women's bodies, already dehumanised and reduced to property, were viewed as something that could be violated, exploited, destroyed, penetrated and subjugated to the most abhorrent, inhumane conditions. The legitimisation of such practices, recognised even by the Catholic Church, resulted in the impossibility of 'raping' Black bodies both legally, due to their status as property, and morally, because their 'animalistic' sexual urges made them always 'ready' for sex.[2]

Brazil, on the other side of the Atlantic, was colonised by the Portuguese and became the epicentre of slavery for 350 years. Historian Emília Viotti da Costa has estimated that 40 per cent of the 10 million trafficked and enslaved Africans ended up in Brazil.[3] Today, the nation has the second-highest demographic proportion of Black people in the world. Consequently, no African country other than Nigeria has more Black people than Brazil. When we consider the implications of slavery and colonisation on the lives of Black women, there are few places where these are felt as brutally as in Brazil, where gender, race and social class all intersect to shape the experience of being a Black woman.

In the 1990s, Kimberlé Crenshaw coined the term 'intersectionality' to broaden and strengthen feminist analysis by exploring sites where gender converges with other characteristics such as ethnicity, class, religion, sexual orientation, identity, disability and age to produce overlapping structures of subordination.[4] This analysis provides a way of recognising that violence towards women usually occurs within specific contexts, varying considerably depending on the woman's identity and social characteristics.

Certain groups of women are thus more likely to experience everyday acts of violence due to the interplay of their gender, ethnic background, religion or social class. In turn, the way these characteristics operate in cultural and political discourses shapes the ways violence against non-white women is both experienced and addressed.

Misogyny is a particular form of violence directed at women, underpinned by 'feelings of hating women or the belief that men are much better than women'.[5] It has its roots in historical power relations between men and women, characterised by the use and abuse of power and control in both public and private spheres. Fundamentally, misogyny is intrinsically linked to gender stereotypes that underline and perpetuate violence against women and girls. As a result, crimes such as domestic abuse, sexual violence, harassment and stalking disproportionately affect women and girls.

Although historically white women's bodies were also objectified and subjugated during the centuries of the slave trade, white women benefited from the structural protection of white supremacy, which meant that their bodies were not treated as disposable. The social construct of whiteness, based on the idea of white supremacy, ensured that Caucasian people had power, privilege and priority, to the extent that it became the 'invisible default', or the norm to which all other people were compared.[6] Interestingly, as illustrated by journalist, author and academic Ruby Hamad, white women who sought to be economically independent from men often found that they were not afforded the same protections as other white women because, although they were not seen as a threat to white supremacy, they certainly challenged the notion of patriarchy.[7]

The idea of the 'generic woman' is similar to that of the 'generic man' in Western philosophy, a concept that is used to refer to both women and men collectively – for example, 'every man is born equal' includes women too. The idea of the generic woman narrows and flattens the great breadth and depth of women's experiences, and the differences between women themselves.[8] Thus, although most of us recognise the ethnic, class, religious and cultural differences among us, we often fail to acknowledge the systemic and interlocking oppressions of colonialism, misogyny and racism. As a result, there is an underlying assumption that the experiences of sexism are separate from those of racism, religious discrimination and the legacies of colonialism. The various aspects of identity are treated as separate atomic particles,[9] as the emphasis on gender tends to downplay the reality that racism and sexism work together to oppress those who experience them.

Intersectionality in feminism provides a way to analyse how misogyny impacts minority women in particular, inter-personal, social and institutional ways, shaping their experience and response to harassment, domestic violence, work and health outcomes globally.

When considering the concept of minority women, it's important to acknowledge that said women might belong to demographic groups that constitute a numerical majority, such as Black women in South Africa or Brazil. Nevertheless, their status as minorities is prescribed by their inability to enjoy full rights as citizens due to historical inequalities. This is known as the concept of 'minorised majorities'.

I personally never felt the experience of being a Black woman quite as intensely as I did when I lived in Brazil. I often say that I became a Black woman in Brazil. Certainly, I was called that everywhere I went – *negra*, *mulata*, *africana*, all words that remind Black women that they were once the property of white men who created names, characteristics and identities for them – and I was *treated* as such everywhere I went too. Even the simple act of taking a residential lift would be both gendered and racialised, as I would be questioned by building security about whether I should take the 'service' lift instead.

For centuries, the West has produced representations of non-white women that came to be accepted as 'more real than the real'.[10] Hamad has emphasised how, historically, characters such as 'Jezebels', 'Black Velvet', 'Gins', 'Harem Girls', 'China Dolls' and 'Princess Pocahontas' were created to stereotype non-white women, and reduce them to sexual objects and caricatures with no agency other than to show adoration for white men. These deeply entrenched notions create cut-out archetypes into which non-white women are still forced to fit, at the same time justifying the attitudes of men who harass women based on the idea that they must always 'want it'.

These conceptions of non-white women were popularised through letters, novels, paintings, human zoos and other depictions that were widely disseminated at the height of the period of colonialism. For instance, the famous French novelist Gustave Flaubert described Egyptian women as 'machines' who did not discriminate when it came to sexual partners, concluding that, as immoral subjects, these women were little more than animal in nature, unlike the superior white European woman.[11]

African women such as Sarah Baartman were exhibited across Europe in human zoos and their bodies were exposed as examples of the undercivilised, animalistic and oversexed nature of Black women. These prejudices were given the veneer of scientific 'objectivity' thanks to European scientists who equated Baartman's anatomical differences with sexual deviance and then drew conclusions about her and other Black women's sexuality. Against the standard for humanity determined by white people in which white bodies became the point of reference, the bodies of all non-white women were considered to be the physical manifestation of their inferiority, and as a result were used to justify the incredible violence inflicted on their bodies.

There is no question that the world has changed considerably in the past fifty or so years. However, very little has changed to challenge asymmetrical sexual relationships between white European men and non-white women. As such, although slavery and colonialism were challenged by successive movements globally, and labour relations have changed, systems of domination have not and the overall dynamics of oppression in society – including the colonial structure of race/class/gender/sexual relations – remain prevalent, particularly in settler colonial societies such as the United States, Brazil, Australia and Canada.

As racism began to be challenged in Western societies in the 1950s and 1960s, with the end of World War II and the subsequent independence movements throughout Asia and Africa, the dichotomy separating white women from all 'otherised' women was transformed. As non-white women could no longer, legally, be raped in impunity, representations of them shifted from depicting merely sexual objects to adding stereotypes such as 'angry Black women', the cold-hearted 'Dragon Asian Ladies', who were accused of using their sexuality to deceive and destroy, and 'Bad Arab' women, who were represented as having their sexuality oppressed. First Nations women around the world continued also to be labelled under colonial slurs as promiscuous,[12] uncaring 'infanticidal cannibals' who did not love their children.[13] So, the transformation in the way non-white women were seen was the addition of further racism and stereotypes that reproduced their dehumanisation and discrimination.

For instance, research has emphasised religion as a crucial determinant in how Muslim women experience misogyny as it intersects with the rise of Islamophobia that followed September 11, 2001, in countries such as the United States and the United Kingdom.[14] Movements such as #MosqueMeToo have become instrumental in highlighting the ways in which Muslim women have been targeted, harassed and assaulted in places of prayer, including during Hajj, the pilgrimage to Mecca that is one of the holiest dates on the Muslim calendar. This violence against Muslim women has been largely ignored by white feminist activism.

Even power and privilege in other spheres is no guarantee of protection against the compounding impact of misogyny and racism. Tennis champion Serena Williams has routinely been the subject of representations with racist undertones that empha- sise her supposedly unwomanly and masculine traits. The 'angry strong Black woman' stereotype is often invoked in negative social media comments about her, describing her as 'a gorilla' or 'more manly than any man'. In 2018, Australian newspaper cartoon- ist Mark Knight faced accusations of sexism and racism for his portrayal of Williams in a style that referenced 'sambo' and Jim Crow–era depictions of Black people. Sociologist Andrew Jakubowicz observed at the time that in Australia there has been a long tradition of cartoons that exaggerate physical characteris- tics of minority groups, including First Nations Australians, with the intention to 'trigger a reaction'.[15] However, the Australian Press

Council found that the cartoon did not breach media standards around 'causing substantial offence, distress or prejudice'.[16]

Both the media that circulate denigrating images of women from minority groups and the standards agencies that legitimise the publication of such images help maintain white supremacy by offering tacit approval of the discriminatory treatment of non-white women in Western societies. As media scholars attest, negative narratives and images do more harm than just affecting the self-esteem of the populations depicted; they materially impact the lives of minority women by justifying the poor treatment they receive across all sectors of society, from education to health and employment as well as online.[17]

Feminist scholar and writer Moya Bailey coined the term 'misogynoir' to describe the ways anti-Black, racist and misogynistic representations shape broader ideas about Black women, particularly in visual culture and digital spaces.[18] As a form of misogyny that is aimed at Black women and is uniquely detrimental to Black women, misogynoir describes a particular brand of hatred directed at Black women.[19] In other words, it is where racism and sexism meet to create particular experiences for Black women. We can see this in the abuse experienced by Black women such as Diane Abbott, a UK member of parliament, and Marielle Franco, a Black, bisexual politician from Brazil who was killed in broad daylight in an act of political violence in Rio de Janeiro in 2018.

As a Black woman from 'the favela' (a type of informal settlement in Brazil), Marielle showed the nation that Black women from the peripheries, intersecting her Blackness, poverty and sexual orientation, could be in politics. She managed to win a seat on the city council, receiving the fifth most votes in the municipality of Rio. Marielle epitomised a struggle, trying to defend her right to be in politics in a country where, in the 2020 local elections, men made up 84 per cent of city councillors elected around the country. Among the 16 per cent of women elected, only 34 per cent of them were Black, while 59 per cent were white women. Thus, for every 100 councillors elected in 2020, only sixteen were women, and only five of those women were non-white.[20] This is despite the fact that Black women comprise the largest demographic group in the country.

Black women in politics in Brazil face enormous challenges and a very hostile environment, including frequent death threats. A study published by the Marielle Franco Institute, an advocacy organisation established in memory of Marielle, in 2021 found that 98.5 per cent of the 142 Black women in elected office who were interviewed reported suffering more than one type of political violence. This ranged from online violence (78 per cent) to moral or psychological (62 per cent) and institutional violence (53 per cent).[21] Unfortunately, it was Marielle's tenacity and boldness in challenging this status quo as a poor Black woman that motivated her death.

Although both Black men and women are the targets of racism in society, misogynoir can also be perpetuated by Black men. For instance, the hashtag #RuinABlackGirlsMonday became a trending topic on Twitter during 2014 and 2015. Posts that featured this tag included images – posted mostly by Black men – that degraded and vilified Black women. The intention was to provoke and convey a specific message to Black women on Twitter, as well as to shame and police Black women and their bodies. The distinctive aspect of this particular negative representation of Black women is that it mainly focused on comparisons between Black women or their characteristics and features and those of white women. Many posts were framed to demonstrate that white women are 'more attractive' and 'less demanding' than black women.[22]

Non-white women continue to be ridiculed through caricatures and stereotypes in film, music, literature and, more recently, social media. They are still seen as lacking the 'womanness' traits of the generic woman. This reinforces the privilege of white, middle class women from Western industrialised countries, as their lives and occupations, griefs and joys come to constitute the norm in relation to which other women's lives are viewed as differing from.[23] White feminism articulates a form of liberal feminism that has a long history interwoven with white privilege, class privilege, colonialism and heteronormativity, and which ignores the structural barriers or systemic biases that hinder gender equality. The intended audience of white feminism can be ignorant or unaccepting of the fact that the historical antecedents of this brand of feminism are rooted in colonialism.[24] As such, it centres a particular kind of woman: middle to upper-middle class, predominantly white, working in corporations, heterosexual, married (or planning to marry) and cisgender.[25]

More than two decades ago, Australian First Nations woman and former magistrate Pat O'Shane was already stressing that women's movements must come to terms with the deep roots of racism within mainstream feminism.[26] Yet, overwhelmingly, there remains a feeling among many non-white feminists that the movement still needs to be held accountable for marginalising the voices and experiences of women from minority groups. Many feel that the type of feminism that finds the loudest voice in mainstream media, often criticised as 'elite' feminism, represents the interests of a small minority of corporate women who celebrate International Women's Day by holding exclusive events that would be out of reach to the majority of women in any given society.

One outcome of this exclusive brand of feminism is that the misogyny experienced by non-white women often goes unreported and unaddressed. In 2021, the kidnapping and murder of 33-year-old marketing executive Sarah Everard in London made international headlines and mobilised thousands of people across the United Kingdom to protest about violence against women. At the time, this was contrasted with the death of Blessing Olusegun, a 21-year-old London-based student and Black woman, whose body was found in September 2020 less than 40 miles from where Everard's body was found months later. Olusegun's death went mostly unreported and unaccounted for.[27] In the United States, the disappearance of Gabby Petito recently gained worldwide coverage, while in Wyoming, the state in which Petito went missing, 710 Indigenous people, mostly girls, have gone missing in the past decade without a single one of them becoming household names or the subject of national news stories.[28]

There are similar stories in Canada, Australia and Brazil, where the killings of Black, Indigenous and other non-white women have not elicited the same public awareness that acts of violence against white women have. This could also be said of violent acts against transgender women versus cisgender women globally. In 2004, American journalist and TV newscaster Gwen Ifill famously coined the term 'missing white woman syndrome' to describe the phenomenon of the extensive and obsessive media coverage of white, middle-class women and girls who have gone missing. Such stories illustrate how physical appearance and ethnicity can be life-or-death determinants in cases of missing persons.

Yet, the data shows that non-white women are more at risk of violence. Global statistics point to 87,000 women intentionally killed in 2017.[29] More than half of them, 58 per cent (50,000), were killed by intimate partners or other family members, meaning that on average, 137 women worldwide are killed by a member of their own family every day. The largest number of all women killed was in Asia (20,000), followed by Africa (19,000), the Americas (8000), Europe (3000) and Oceania (300). Although the largest number was in Asia, women and girls run the greatest risk of being killed by an intimate partner or other family member in Africa.[30]

The position of non-white women in society is directly impacted by broader contexts of discrimination, such as colonial domination, continued marginalisation, poverty, limited access to social services, dispossession from ancestral lands and issues of militarisation, which simultaneously heighten women's vulnerability to violence and limit their ability to seek protection and recourse. Therefore, misogyny against these women cannot be separated from colonial legacies and the wider contexts of prejudice and exclusion to which non-white people as a whole are often exposed in social, political, economic and cultural life.

For instance, in Australia, the overlapping constructs of sexism, racism and false notions of white supremacy mean that First Nations women are relegated to the lowest level of the Eurocentric default of society. Because of this, First Nations women are frequently undervalued within professional contexts and under-represented in senior roles.[31] This then perpetuates the cycle of oppressions, as their voices are largely absent from decision-making processes governed by Western and patriarchal systems of control.

The statistics are stark. Between 2010 and 2014, despite representing only around 3.3 per cent of the Australian female population, First Nations women were 32 times more likely to be hospitalised and eleven times more likely to die due to assault than non-Indigenous women.[32] The police and the justice system are often seen as themselves structurally violent and therefore unable to protect Indigenous women. This extends also to sexual assault and workplace harassment, as First Nations women often do not feel welcome or safe to report sexual harassment, for fear of being victim-blamed by colleagues who may already resent them because of the misguided belief that First Nations people only get jobs because of affirmative action.[33] The unique experiences of First Nations women, and the way racism impacts their lived experiences, are often silenced by white feminists, who can be complicit in the perpetuation of myths and stereotypes linked to colonial legacies.

In Canada, a similar crisis is ongoing, with a conservative estimate that there are 1100 missing and murdered Indigenous women and girls around the country. The systemic and interlocking oppressions of colonialism, misogyny and racism were all identified as root causes of the crisis.[34] Indigenous women aged 25 to 44 are five times more likely than other Canadian women in the same age range to die as a result of violence, twelve times more likely to be murdered or go missing than members of any other demographic group and sixteen times more likely to disappear or to be slain than white women.[35]

Alongside technological innovations and our increased participation in digital spaces, the abuse targeted at women has also moved to online formats. Colonialism, sexism and racism are as present in digital spaces as they are in any other space, and the digital dimension of misogyny can also have a serious impact on the lives of women and girls, including their safety, psychological and physical health, livelihoods, family ties, dignity and reputation. The violence that women can experience online can be particularly harmful for minority women, who are at risk of or exposed to intersecting forms of violence. For example, globally, Black women are 84 per cent more likely to receive abusive messages on Twitter than other women.[36]

Research suggests that those groups that are more vulnerable to harassment offline, such as women and non-white people in general, are also more likely to be targeted online.[37] A survey conducted by the organisation HateAid found that around 52 per cent of women aged 18 to 35 have suffered digital violence at least once. Women from a migrant background were particularly likely to be affected by threats, abuse and slander online.[38] There is evidence of Roma women in North Macedonia being particularly targeted by certain Facebook pages, on which users post disparaging comments about them, as well as private and explicit photos and videos.[39]

In the United Kingdom, Black, Asian and Minority Ethnic (BAME) women MPs are far more likely to receive abuse on social media than their white colleagues. A study by Amnesty International found that in the run-up to the 2017 UK general election, twenty BAME MPs received almost half (40 per cent) of the abusive tweets sent, despite there being almost eight times as many white MPs in the group examined by the study.[40]

One woman, Diane Abbott – who was the United Kingdom's first Black female MP and is the current Labour MP for Hackney North and Stoke Newington – receives an incredibly disproportionate amount of online abuse, and was the target of almost one-third (31.61 per cent) of all the abusive tweets analysed by the Amnesty International study. The abuse Abbott receives often centres on her race and ethnicity, and includes threats of sexual violence. She reported being sent postcards and letters with pictures of monkeys and chimps, as well as hundreds of emails using the word 'n*****' and calling her a prostitute. In the six weeks leading up to the 2017 election, 45.14 per cent of all abusive tweets were aimed at her, amounting to an average of 51 abusive tweets per day over the 158-day study.[41] Diane Abbott's experience illustrates the unique combination of racialised and sexist violence that befalls Black women as a result of their simultaneous and linked oppression at the intersection of racial and gender marginalisation.[42]

At the same time that non-white women are more frequently targeted by online abuse, the online space is also emerging as a site of resistance and solidarity. Women can unite with each other on a global scale, using their collective power to speak out and amplify their voices both online and offline. The digital sphere has allowed minorities to create new spaces in ways that traditional platforms such as the mainstream media did not afford, allowing them to create and share content, as well as fundraise for grassroots causes. It has also enabled non-white women to mobilise against the exclusivity of white feminism. For instance, in August 2013, author and activist Mikki Kendall started the hashtag #SolidarityIsForWhiteWomen as a form of cyber-feminist activism directed at the lack of action by white feminists who fail to acknowledge the specificities of the racist and sexist targeting of non-white women.[43]

Researcher Kishonna L. Gray has suggested that in recent years intersectionality has gone 'viral' as social media has proven to be an innovative arena in which to express individual and collective experiences of misogyny as felt by historically marginalised people. Examples include trending hashtags such as #SayHerName,

#FastTailedGirls, #NotYourAsianSidekick, #NotYourMami and #MMIW (missing and murdered Indigenous women). These examples of digital feminist activism embody the physical and online experiences of racialised women, who now can employ digital technologies to democratise information sharing, raise awareness and create new spheres of resistance and empowerment, using an intersectional approach.[44] Ultimately, this contributes to increased solidarity among all women, which is crucial in the fight back against misogynistic behaviour.

In this chapter I have drawn on intersectionality to examine the particularities of the misogyny that is directed at non-white women across different contexts. In doing so, I hope to have illustrated that treating women as a homogeneous group does more harm than good, as the experiences of non-white women often go unaccounted for and unaddressed. The advent of the internet has created new opportunities, as social media plays an important role in giving voice to those traditionally silenced by various systems of oppression. I am thus hopeful that the next ten years will build on the progress that we have made and lay the foundations for the radical changes that we need to see in our societies.

'What's the worst misogyny you've had to deal with in your career?' Responses from *A Podcast of One's Own*

When I was running for office on the board of the [Alabama] state medical society, which controlled all of health care in the state, you had to go around to different groups and speak to them. And I went to one and there was this doctor who said, 'Who is going with you?' and he volunteered to go with me. He was an older doctor who took me under his wing and would introduce me to people. We went into a room and this one doctor stood up and, talking to the older doctor, he said, 'Now, Bill, this ain't right. We don't need a black person on this board. Besides, we got one woman anyway.' The older doctor was going to answer, and I said, 'No, I'll answer.' And I explained that I wasn't running as a black person and I wasn't running as a woman, I was running as the most qualified person, and if he didn't think I was the most qualified then he should vote for someone else – and then I went on with my speech. Well, this same guy became one of my strongest supporters throughout the years. Understand, that was what he believed at the time and it often takes time to change one's beliefs.

Regina Benjamin, former Surgeon General of the United States

The tone of Question Time is set by the headlines of the day, and the reports of Slipper's texts meant this day was going to be a doozy. I was readying myself for the onslaught.

But what followed was a calm; a calm of outrage from a prime minister who had every right to be offended.

You could feel that the speech was having an impact – flawless delivery, decrying of hypocrisy, unflinching, silencing the usual cacophony of noise. My crowd control skills were barely required.

I was concentrating so hard on managing the behaviour in the House, I couldn't have told you what the prime minister said, but I can say it was fascinating to watch the opposition go from elation to deflation, and to see the relief on the government's front bench.

Anna Burke, *former Australian Member of Parliament for Chisholm and Speaker of the House of Representatives*

Chapter 6

Sexism today: Tools in the patriarchy's toolbox

Michelle K. Ryan and Miriam K. Zehnter

It is misogyny, sexism, every day from this Leader of the Opposition. Every day, in every way, across the time the Leader of the Opposition has sat in that chair and I have sat in this chair, that is all we have heard from him.

As Julia Gillard's speech demonstrates, misogyny and sexism go hand in hand. While misogyny is relatively simply defined – as hatred of, or entrenched prejudice against, women[1] – sexism is a more complex, nuanced and multifaceted beast. This is in part because sexism is no one single thing, but rather a constellation of attitudes, beliefs and behaviours that reinforce patriarchal systems of gender inequality in society. To illustrate the range of these attitudes, beliefs and behaviours, we can think of the many forms of sexism as different tools within the patriarchy's toolbox.

Before we can defeat these forms of sexism and misogyny, we need to be able to identify them and understand how they work.

To this end, we will explore the many faces of sexism, from the blatant to the subtle, the intentional to the inadvertent and the hostile to the more 'benevolent'. We will look at how individuals might strategically wield different types of sexism, in different contexts, to different ends. We will also demonstrate that the common thread running through these actions is that sexist attitudes, beliefs and behaviours are tools that are brought out to keep women and gender minority groups 'in their place' and to reinforce the status quo.

First, though: what is sexism? It might feel like one of those concepts that is hard to put into words, but we all know it when we see it, right? However, the definition of sexism is actually a contested space. Some people argue we should have a broad view of sexism that incorporates a whole range of behaviours, from overt discrimination to unconscious microaggressions and systems that result in disadvantages for women. The Everyday Sexism Project, for example, provides a platform where women can report the wide variety of sexism they encounter, from mundane day-to-day interactions to hostile attacks.[2] But there are others who feel that such breadth goes too far – arguing that if you label everything as sexism, then you dilute the power of the word to call things out. This difficulty in describing sexism only makes it harder to combat.

If we want to get more formal with our definitions, in 2019, the Council of Europe, the continent's leading human rights organisation, developed the first internationally agreed upon definition of sexism:

Any act, gesture, visual representation, spoken or written words, practice or behaviour based upon the idea that a person or a group of persons is inferior because of their sex, which occurs in the public or private sphere, whether online or offline, with the purpose or effect of:

- violating the inherent dignity or rights of a person or a group of persons; or
- resulting in physical, sexual, psychological or socio-economic harm or suffering to a person or a group of persons; or
- creating an intimidating, hostile, degrading, humiliating or offensive environment; or
- constituting a barrier to the autonomy and full realisation of human rights by a person or a group of persons; or
- maintaining and reinforcing gender stereotypes.[3]

The American Psychological Association expands upon this definition by including beliefs and attitudes as well as actions and behaviours, and acknowledging that sexism can be subtle and can occur at multiple levels, from the individual to in society more generally:

Sexism is associated with acceptance of sex-role stereotypes and can occur at multiple levels: individual, organizational, institutional, and cultural. It may be overt, involving the open endorsement of sexist beliefs or attitudes; covert, involving the tendency to hide sexist beliefs or attitudes and reveal them only when it is believed that one will not suffer publicly for them; or subtle, involving unequal treatment that may not be noticed because it is part of everyday behavior or perceived to be unimportant.[4]

Our view, as psychologists who specialise in sexism and gender inequality, is that, rather than focusing on pinning down a precise definition of what sexism *is*, we should concentrate on defining what it is that sexism *does*. Although sexism manifests in many different forms, what each form has in common is that it sustains the gendered status quo in specific ways.

It is important to acknowledge that sexism experienced at an interpersonal level is a problem in society and can impact people's perceptions of their safety, confidence, health and wellbeing. This is of course compounded for people facing intersectional forms of discrimination, such as racism or homophobia. But it is also important to consider the systemic effects of sexism, and how they play out in organisations and in society more generally – that is, that sexism is a key factor in reinforcing women's individual and social disadvantages. As an illustration of this, research conducted across 57 countries shows very clearly that sexist attitudes held by individuals directly and causally exacerbate the disparities between women and men, and create and maintain gender inequality within their broader society.[5]

We can look to evidence from the field of social psychology to distinguish between different forms of sexism and their functions. Social psychology is a useful perspective to take, because as a discipline it is concerned with how attitudes and behaviours (such as sexism) are shaped by other individuals, by groups and by society more broadly; and with the effects these attitudes and behaviours have on social interactions and social structures. To date, the most studied forms of sexism have been **traditional sexism**, a concept developed in the 1970s, and **hostile sexism**, **benevolent sexism** and **modern sexism**, which were all described in the 1990s. But we can also look at emerging forms of sexism that are rearing their head today, such as **belief in sexism shift**, which was first described in 2020.

When people think about sexism, what most commonly comes to mind are the more traditional forms of sexism. Sometimes called 'old-fashioned sexism', such sexism is blatant, and based on the notion that women are simply inferior to men: less able, less rational, less ambitious, less moral. Women and girls were (and in some circles still are) seen not to have the intelligence, temperament or the need to be as educated as men and boys. These supposed deficits were (and are) used to justify the exclusion of women from many facets of society, including politics, the workplace and other spheres of power and influence. Individuals who hold such traditionally sexist attitudes believe that intellectual and leadership roles should be left to men, while women should concern themselves with housekeeping and the upbringing of children.

Julia Gillard gives a vivid example of traditional sexism in the misogyny speech:

> I was also very offended on behalf of the women of Australia when in the course of the carbon pricing campaign the Leader of the Opposition said, 'What the housewives of Australia need to understand as they do the ironing.' Thank you for that painting of women's roles in modern Australia!

While such traditionally sexist attitudes clearly persist to this day, they have been shown to have decreased over time. Today, openly advocating against women's right to vote, or for the gender segregation of work, would be considered not just 'politically incorrect' or not 'woke', but completely out of step with modern times. While the true prevalence of sexism in society is difficult to quantify, our recent research looks to measure levels of sexism in the workplace, a context that shapes many of our lives and one where men and women frequently interact. We found that, on average, working women in the United Kingdom believe 27 per cent of their colleagues hold traditionally sexist views, such that men should be breadwinners and women should be homemakers. In male-dominated workplaces, this increases to 57 per cent.[6] The contemporary presence of traditional sexism is also reflected in the fact that women in heterosexual relationships take on more household and parenting tasks, even if they work equal or longer hours in professional jobs than their male partners.[7]

As a tool, traditional sexism functions like a mould, trying to preserve the shape of the gendered status quo as it once was. The consequences of traditional sexism are palpable. Individuals who espouse traditionally sexist beliefs have more positive attitudes towards men in general – particularly male chauvinists (that is, men who believe their own gender to be superior). They also have more virulent attitudes towards women in general – particularly towards feminist women.[8] These attitudes can be seen as a backlash directed towards women who dare to step outside the traditional mould – such as women who work in male-dominated roles or professions, those in leadership positions, or those who work in STEM (science, technology, engineering and mathematics) or the military.

Working in an environment where traditional sexism is entrenched can have a severe negative impact on women's health and wellbeing. Indeed, our research shows that the greater the proportion of colleagues believed to hold traditionally sexist views, the higher women's self-reported levels of depression and burnout symptoms will be.[9] At its most extreme, traditional sexism, and the associated backlash against women seen to flout its conventions, contributes to violence against women in intimate heterosexual relationships, including psychological and physical abuse as well as cyberbullying.[10] Among women and men, traditionally sexist views are also associated with increased victim blaming and decreased blaming of the perpetrator in instances of rape.[11]

Another form of blatant sexism is 'hostile sexism'.[12] Hostile sexism is often directed towards non-traditional and feminist women, and women with power, especially if they use that power to promote a feminist agenda. In this way, hostile sexism is fundamentally antagonistic, and regards women as being controlling or manipulative. When psychologists measure hostile sexism, we ask people to indicate their agreement with statements such as, 'When women lose to men in a fair competition, they typically complain about being discriminated against', and 'Many women are actually seeking special favours, such as hiring policies that favour them over men, under the guise of asking for equality'. Agreement with such sentiments reveals a certain reactiveness to change and to the successes of feminism.

Abusive language, such as 'Ditch the witch' and 'a man's bitch' quoted in the misogyny speech, is an overt example of hostile sexism. Plentiful examples of hostile sexism can also be found in online environments on a daily basis in the form of trolling and abuse directed at prominent women, especially towards those who come forward with allegations of violence and harassment. In terms of prevalence, our research shows working women in the United Kingdom believe that, on average, 20 per cent of their colleagues hold hostile sexist views. In male-dominated professions, this rises to 40 per cent of colleagues.[13] A study conducted among US college students found that even in the relatively progressive environment of a college campus, women experienced, on average, one incidence of hostile sexism per week.[14] These numbers are concerning.

Indeed, the adverse consequences of hostile sexism for women are well documented. Those who endorse hostile sexism perceive women to be less competent than men and see the gender wage gap as being justified.[15] Hostile sexists have a higher tolerance of sexual harassment in the workplace, and downplay the severity and the expected negative consequences for victims of sexual harassment.[16] Men who demonstrate high levels of hostile sexist beliefs think that women who experience harassment should refrain from reporting or confronting it and ignore it instead. They are also more likely to victim-blame and to perceive harassers in a positive light.[17] Tragically, as we saw with traditional sexism, the more men agree with hostile sexism, the more likely they are to engage in violence against women, including psychological and physical abuse,[18] cyberbullying,[19] and even rape.[20]

With all this in mind, it is not surprising that working with colleagues who endorse hostile sexism impacts women's mental health significantly, again increasing the risk of depression and burnout.[21] Merely observing hostility against other women at work hurts women's professional self-esteem and reduces their career aspirations.[22] Even though feminist women are the most likely targets of hostile sexism, attacks on feminist women are problematic for all women because they have a silencing effect. Concerns about repercussions can discourage women from doing things that may be construed as feminist, such as standing up to gender discrimination and reporting sexual harassment.[23] In this way, hostile sexism functions as a tool for pushing back against progress, getting women 'back in their box' and stymieing change.

While it has become increasingly unacceptable in the twenty-first century to voice blatantly sexist attitudes, we have seen that such sexism is still very much a part of our society. But some of the especially insidious tools in the patriarchy's toolbox are the less overt forms of sexism that are more difficult to clearly recognise as sexist. This includes subtler manifestations of traditional sexism, and one of the most studied forms of sexism, 'benevolent sexism' – or, paternalistic attitudes towards women who do not challenge traditional gender roles.

Subtle traditional sexism, like its more blatant counterpart, works to reinforce the status quo by advocating for intellectual and leadership roles to be in the hands of men, and household and child-rearing roles in the hands of women. Rather than being expressed openly, this view tends to be hidden behind seemingly benign concern for others – the classic 'Won't someone think of the children!' approach.[24] As such, subtle traditional sexism typically makes appeals to the welfare of children – who are believed to suffer from the absence of their working mothers – or even to the unborn – who are perceived to be sacrificed in exchange for the freedom of women to pursue their careers.

Our recent research suggests that subtle traditional sexism is incredibly widespread. On average, working women reported that 40 per cent of their colleagues believe that it's best for small children if their mothers stay at home as much as possible.[25] There is clear evidence that women commonly face subtle traditional sexism: for example, female employees, especially those at senior levels, report being regularly lectured by their colleagues about the presumed negative impact of their career choices on their children. These critiques are most frequently delivered by men, many of whom themselves have children who are presumably looked after by their female partners or by paid childcare workers.[26]

As a tool, subtle traditional sexism seeks to make sexist views appear harmless by packaging them in concerns for others. However, this expression of sexism is often insidiously effective, as it plays on fears held by many women – 'Am I a good mother?' 'What if my work *does* disadvantage my child?' And sexism disguised as seemingly well-intended concern for children can negatively impact women who do not have children, too, by promoting stress about one's 'biological clock', triggering painful emotions about one's personal situation or anxiety over unfulfilled wishes, or causing concern that one's life choices are being condemned as 'unnatural'.

The potential harm subtle traditional sexism can do is particularly evident when people's concern for others is directed towards unborn life rather than living women. In Australia, about 90,000 women have an abortion per year.[27] In the United States, on average, one in four women will have an abortion within their lifetime.[28] Not even considering that abortion rights are persistently under threat even in a progressive country like the United States, having relatively easy access to abortions does not necessarily make the decision or experience an easy one. As a consequence, comments such as 'Abortion is the easy way out', as was quoted in the misogyny speech, not only imply that bearing children is the appropriate role for women, they also use some of the most complex and personal decisions a person can make – about whether and under what circumstances to have children – to ostracise women from the world of work and remind them of their traditional role in society. As a tool, subtle traditional sexism is the stealthier version of traditional sexism's mould – it demarcates a space and a place for women not by direct decree, but through concerned appeal about the wellbeing of others. Its subtlety is its power.

We have seen that hostile sexism punishes women who step outside of traditional gender roles; we can think of 'benevolent sexism' as the other side of the coin to hostile sexism. As a tool, benevolent sexism operates as a reward system, to incentivise women who conform to traditional roles.[29] In the eyes of those who endorse benevolent sexism, women are seen to be worthy of protection but not as fully competent adults. Benevolent sexism builds on the 'women-are-wonderful' stereotype, a trend demonstrated in psychological and sociological research that shows people tend to idolise women as being morally superior to men.[30] Benevolent sexism may, on the surface, seem rather chivalrous, but it arises from a paternalistic attitude that assumes women are weak and need to be protected. In this way, it is a stealthy tool to use, cloaking a view that women are less than equal under the guise of suggesting they are 'special'. It is noteworthy, though, that this protection is most likely to be extended to white women and less likely afforded to women of colour.[31]

Although some women may benefit from or even welcome benevolent sexism, its foundation lies in stereotypical and restrictive views of women and what constitutes a 'womanly' demeanour.[32] As a result, double standards are applied to the behaviour of women and men. This can result in a 'Don't worry your pretty little head about it' attitude, where the 'protection' of women from danger or difficult circumstances is used to justify their exclusion – exclusion from particular jobs and roles, exclusion from decision-making, and a loss of autonomy. There were shades of benevolent sexism when Prime Minister Tony Abbott called his Deputy Prime Minister, Julie Bishop, 'a loyal girl', emphasising her place in relationship to him while at the same time using belittling, infantilising language.[33]

Although the subtle nature of benevolent sexism makes it different to more overt or hostile forms of sexism, the endorsement of such attitudes has been shown to go hand in hand with other forms of sexism. Benevolent sexist attitudes are also associated with opposition to women's reproductive rights, including negative views of birth control and abortion access.[34] On one hand, benevolent sexism glorifies motherhood; on the other hand, it holds women to a higher moral standard than men and expects them to place their professional and personal needs and aspirations second. In the workplace, those who hold benevolent sexist views are also likely to perceive women as less competent than men and hold negative attitudes towards women in male-dominated professions.[35] While men who demonstrate high levels of benevolent sexist beliefs tend to behave in a friendly manner towards their female co-workers,[36] they assign fewer challenging experiences to women, even if women express equal interest in such experiences.[37] Figuratively speaking, while benevolent sexists will hold some doors open for women, at other times they will fail to invite them in to the room where real decision-making happens. In this way, they undermine women's career progress while keeping a friendly face.

The subtlety of benevolent sexism makes it in many ways the most challenging form of sexism to confront. Because it comes wrapped in a packaging of chivalry, protection and the potentially flattering ascription of moral superiority, women can have a hard time recognising and calling out benevolent sexism as being sexist.[38] As a consequence, women tend to internalise the belittling and other negative messages sent through benevolent sexism.

Imagine a woman who works as a software engineer. Her male colleagues mean well when they explain how things are done and offer their help. Their behaviour may be completely appropriate and genuinely helpful in some circumstances, such as when she is new to the job. But imagine that she has worked as a software engineer for a long time. Not recognising her colleagues' excessive helpful behaviour as an expression of sexism, she could wonder whether it's her. She may fear that her colleagues offer their help because she does not have sufficient competence to perform the job on her own. Indeed, research shows that after being treated with benevolent sexism, women have intrusive thoughts about their competence, and these thoughts are so distracting that they then perform poorly on cognitive tasks.[39] Moreover, women who are in romantic relationships with benevolent sexist men have been demonstrated to have lower self-esteem than women who are partnered with non-sexist men.[40]

Whether blatant or subtle, the forms of sexism we have introduced until now all circle around attitudes and beliefs about women and their roles in society that legitimise existing gender inequalities and downplay the need for change. Fundamental to these forms of sexism is 'gender essentialism' – the belief that women and men are fundamentally different physiologically, psychologically or both. Importantly, these differences are argued to have a biological basis and therefore to be unchangeable.[41] In the workplace, gender essentialists often claim that the lack of women in certain roles or sectors is not a product of gender discrimination, but rather is due to women's and men's different natures, needs and talents. One well-publicised example of gender essentialist beliefs is found in a memo written by a former software engineer at Google, who argued that it is women's lower ambition and stress tolerance, and higher neuroticism – not sexism – that explains why they continue to be under-represented in the tech industry.[42] Such essentialist arguments are often followed by the conclusion that efforts to increase women's representation in particular sectors or particular roles, such as leadership, are fruitless, as women by nature are incapable of adapting to such circumstances.

Julia Gillard recounts an expression of gender essentialism in the misogyny speech:

> Then a discussion ensued and another person being inter-viewed said, 'I want my daughter to have as much opportunity as my son,' to which the Leader of the Opposition said: 'Yes, I completely agree, but what if men are by physiology or temperament more adapted to exercise authority or to issue command?

Conceptually, gender essentialism can be seen as part of the foundation on which sexism is built. In other words, gender essentialism is not necessarily a form of sexism in itself, but the notion that women are fundamentally and unchangingly differ-ent from men is a precondition for belief in women's inferiority. To continue the metaphor of this chapter, if sexism is the patri-archy's toolbox, then gender essentialism can be seen as the key to opening it. The existence of the key does not necessarily lead to sexism; indeed, people may believe that while women and men are very different from one another, these differences should be equally valued. It is also noteworthy that gender essentialism does not only open the possibility of sexism, but is also the foun-dation of other forms of discrimination such as gendered racism and transphobia.

Recent data support the idea that gender essentialism is a foundational concept of sexism. Working women in the United Kingdom indicated that, on average, they believe as many as 61 per cent of their colleagues agree with gender essentialism. Given that the perceived prevalence of the different types of sexism ranged between 17 per cent (for belief in sexism shift, which we will look at below) and 40 per cent (for subtle traditional sexism), these numbers suggest that not everyone who endorses gender essentialism endorses sexism. However, the same data also indicated that belief in gender essentialism very much co-occurs with the endorsement of sexist views.[43]

Importantly, individuals often present their ideas about gender essentialism as indisputable scientific facts, and dismiss those – often, feminists – who contradict their pseudoscientific claims as being 'irrational' (an insult that is frequently thrown at women, along with 'emotional'). However, researchers from a variety of fields have found that sorting humans into simple binary categories of women and men is not particularly helpful;[44] that women and men are overall more similar than different;[45] and that many differences are a product of gendered socialisation.[46] Neuroscientists have produced much evidence showing that gender differences in the brain are marginal at best, in contrast to popularly held views about the 'female brain' or the 'male brain'.[47] Endocrinologists have demonstrated that both women and men have so-called 'female' and 'male' sex hormones, and that if one wishes to sort humans into two categories based on hormonal differences, there should be one category with people who are not pregnant, and a second category with people who are pregnant.[48] Finally, psychologists have shown that many behaviours commonly attributed to evolutionary differences are in fact based on differences in socialisation. Take for example sexual behaviour: contrary to the stereotypes of the pro-miscuous, risk-taking man and the monogamous, risk-avoidant woman, women tend to show similar sexual behaviour when the context allows it. Specifically, the higher the gender equality in a country, the freer women are to live out their sexuality.[49]

Despite the continued existence of these overt and more subtle forms of sexism, society has made great gains towards gender equality. But this change itself has resulted in new forms of sexism as a direct backlash against progress, including 'modern sexism' – the denial of ongoing discrimination against women – and a belief that the tables have turned and sexism now disadvantages men rather than women, which is known as 'belief in sexism shift'. Notably, these forms of sexism represent new and unique additions to the patriarchy's toolbox. They are tools unlike any we have seen before. In contrast to the manifestations of sexism we have described so far, these emerging forms of sexism are not concerned with women's attributes or roles in society, but rather centre on the current state of gender discrimination. These new forms of sexism are presented as a comment on or concern about gender equality, which makes them especially subtle and difficult to recognise.

One response to the changes in equality of the sexes is what psychologists call 'modern sexism', which is defined as the denial of discrimination against women.[50] While modern sexism does not explicitly degrade or belittle women, denying the existence of any ongoing discrimination against women has important conse-quences. One consequence is that it places the blame for continuing gender inequalities on women themselves, in particular on their 'lack of abilities or interest'. This is a common justification given when those who deny ongoing discrimination against women are asked to explain why women continue to be under-represented in positions of power. They suggest that women are not as interested in leadership as men, that women lack the ambition to pursue political office, and sometimes even that women do not have the 'masculine' attributes required to be successful managers or leaders. Research has shown that none of this is true.[51]

Modern sexism is an effective tool because, in taking a different approach and shifting the blame, it becomes less obvious and more difficult to recognise as sexism. However, it often goes hand in hand with the more blatant, traditional sexism. Julia Gillard's speech provides a vivid example of this:

> In a discussion about women being under-represented in institutions of power in Australia, the interviewer was a man called Stavros and the Leader of the Opposition said: 'If it's true, Stavros, that men have more power, generally speaking, than women, is that a bad thing?'

Here, the expression of traditional sexism – 'is that a bad thing?', questioning whether women belong in institutions of power – co-occurs with an expression of modern sexism – 'If it's true', casting doubt on whether women are under-represented at all.

Modern sexism is a prevalent form of sexism. In our research into working women in the United Kingdom, subjects reported that 38 per cent of their colleagues agree with modern sexism. Women in more male-dominated professions indicated that about half of their colleagues deny that discrimination against women is still a problem.[52] Cynically, those who negate the existence of anti-female discrimination often go on to do just that.

Research demonstrates that those who endorse modern sexism are more likely to discriminate against women, more likely to rely on men to achieve results, and more likely to rate women as less deserving and less likely to be successful.[53] Women are aware of these contradictions, and research shows that observing modern sexism decreases women's sense of control over their future career decisions and increases their intention of leaving their careers.[54]

Denying the existence of anti-female discrimination also has consequences for policy and practice. To claim, as modern sexism does, that discrimination against women has ended is effectively to argue that further initiatives for the advancement of women are unnecessary or even unfair. Those who espouse modern sexist beliefs perceive gender quotas for leadership positions to be unnecessary and unmeritocratic.[55] Among women themselves, modern sexist beliefs have been shown to reduce anger about gendered inequalities and lower the intention to support or engage in collective action, such as protests.[56]

The final type of sexism we will explore is perhaps the newest form to be identified – 'belief in sexism shift'. This tool is characterised by the belief that men have become the primary victims of sexism, that male victimisation is pervasive and that this new form of discrimination is the direct result of women's societal advancement. As its name suggests, those who endorse this view perceive there has been a shift or transition from anti-female sexism to anti-male sexism.[57] Proponents of this view believe the shift to have occurred recently, within the past decade or so, and that it has increased to the point where men now suffer more discrimination than women.[58] In this view men are not merely seen as victims of rigid gender norms, alongside women, but rather as the primary targets of gender discrimination.

One prominent example of the belief in sexism shift is the 'Don't mancriminate' campaign in India – a series of videos and posters produced by the Indian online fashion and lifestyle magazine Maggcom, claiming that men, not women, are the true victims of gender discrimination.[59] The campaign produced posters claiming that men are discriminated against by women-only train compartments (which were introduced after the horrendous rape and killing of a twelve-year-old girl that took place on a train), women's claims to child support, women's beauty products, free entry for women into nightclubs and so on. According to the campaign, discrimination against men can be seen everywhere – even in a country that was ranked 140 out of 156 in the 2021 Global Gender Gap Report.[60]

Individuals who endorse the belief in sexism shift perceive anti-male discrimination to be ubiquitous, manifesting in multiple settings (the workplace, politics), through multiple perpetrators (the media, feminists), and in multiple ways (political correctness, devaluation of masculinity, et cetera).

Although belief in sexism shift is ostensibly focused on men, it nevertheless constitutes a form of sexism against women. In this case, negative attitudes towards women are masked behind a narrative of male victimhood in which men's disadvantages are the product of a system that has relentlessly favoured women. By implying that women's progress has been attained through preferential treatment, this belief discounts women's abilities and downplays their merits in their own advancement. Like other forms of sexism, belief in sexism shift sustains the status quo, but it does so by diverting attention from ongoing discrimination against women and redirecting the focus towards men and an ostensibly anti-male system.[61] This diversion is painfully manifest in hashtags such as #HimToo and #NotAllMen that emerged as reactions to #MeToo and women's outcry over widespread sexual harassment and rape culture.

The belief in sexism shift is a recent and, it seems, growing form of sexism. Reflecting its emerging relevance, in 2016 the American National Election Studies – an organisation that administers research-focused surveys of registered voters in the United States – started to ask people about their experiences with anti-male discrimination. Since then, the belief that men are discriminated against more than women has gained popularity, especially among conservatives.[62] Data from research indicate that men in particular believe they are more likely than ever before to suffer gender-based discrimination. Around two-thirds of men claim to have faced at least some discrimination due to their gender.[63]

Women have also been shown to share a belief in sexism shift. In the United States, 9 per cent of women (and 15 per cent of men) believe that women have better job opportunities than men,[64] and 5 per cent of women (and 14 per cent of men) think it is now easier to be a woman than a man.[65] In our research, working women in the United Kingdom indicated that 17 per cent of their colleagues believe that today, discrimination against men exceeds discrimination against women.[66]

Although studies have shown evidence of the belief in sexism shift, little research has examined its consequences given it is still a relatively new phenomenon. However, belief in sexism shift provides an unprecedented rationale for prioritising men's rights over women's rights. From the perspective of those who believe in the shift, efforts to attain gender equality should in effect move away from women's issues to instead focus solely on the protection of men's rights. This may result in the rejection of policies that support women, while embracing the same policies for men. Belief in sexism shift may also foster the rise of highly misogynistic fringe groups, such as 'incels' (short for 'involuntary celibate') and 'Proud Boys' (a US-based far-right, neo-fascist and exclusively male organisation that promotes and engages in political violence). Though these may be extreme examples, supporters of these movements often espouse beliefs that are in line with the belief in sexism shift.[67]

Now that we've outlined these major tools in the patriarchy's toolbox and the way they manifest, we must turn to the important question of what we can do about it. How can we reduce the effectiveness of these forms of sexism in maintaining gender inequalities in our society? Each form of sexism can be seen as a tool with quite a specific purpose, which can be selected depending on what is needed – an attack to put a woman back in her place, some gentle coaxing to convince women to take on increased caring roles, a justification for continuing inequalities or a reason why interventions for women's advancement should not be supported.

It's also possible to find examples where the tools are used together. Professor Jennifer Freyd of the University of Oregon identified what she calls the 'DARVO' technique, which is used by perpetrators of wrongdoing (such as sexual offenders) in response to being called out for their behaviour. DARVO stands for 'Deny, Attack and Reverse Victim and Offender'.[68] With our understanding of the tools in the sexism toolbox, we can see how the various forms of sexism could be used to this end: first, deny sexism exists by employing modern sexist beliefs; then attack, using hostile sexism; and then, finally, reverse the roles of victim and offender through the belief in sexism shift.

The many forms of sexism mean that it is sometimes hard to label sexist behaviour as such, and the ability to switch from one tool to another makes it harder to defend against them. But there are ways forward. First, much of sexism's power comes from its subtlety – that invisible 'glass' in the glass ceiling – and it is not always easy to spot it as it is happening. Having an understanding of how subtle forms of sexism may manifest, and what the person using the tool may be trying to achieve, can make it easier for both women and men to point the finger and call out the sexism when it arises. Second, one needs to have an evidence base ready to combat sexist claims – whether it is evidence that speaks against gender essentialist views of difference, counters modern sexist denials of continuing gender inequalities, or clarifies that inequalities men may face are not a result of women's advancement but are instead the flip side of the same patriarchal coin that creates disadvantage for women.

Here, again, we can see the power of Julia Gillard's misogyny speech. She pointed a finger squarely at sexism in all its forms, tools that were wielded against her personally and against the women of Australia, and in doing so helped to blunt their power. While few of us will ever speak from such a powerful platform as Julia did, the misogyny speech shows how meaningful calling out sexism and misogyny can be. If we continue this calling out with our own voices, collectively, we may just have the same impact.

'What's the worst misogyny you've ever had to face?' Responses from *A Podcast of One's Own*

Online! Particularly on Twitter, where you get people who are nowhere near their real names. The ease with which you get a line of criticism of you about your job, or something that you've written – which is entirely fair enough, you know, every journalist should be prepared to be criticised and, even if it stings, listen to it and respond to it if you want to. But what shocks me is the speed with which it turns into 'You're a slut'. The sexualised nature of it just absolutely stuns me sometimes, and I think that what you see online is often people trying to injure or damage someone that they are frustrated with or are criticising. And the fact that when people are trying to damage or catch the attention of or hurt a female person, the speed with which they repair to some sort of sexualised threat or shaming is just stunning. It really is.

Annabel Crabb, Australian political journalist,
commentator and television host

When I first heard the speech, I had just taken a maternity leave break from my work with a movement of rural young women across Africa who defy the odds stacked against them to achieve an education, with support from CAMFED. I was also reading for my Master of Laws degree. Julia's speech gave me energy to persevere with my studies, knowing that only education can give a woman the power to challenge societal problems, patriarchy and misogyny as Julia had done in the Australian parliament. I thought, if one woman leader can show the world how it is done, we can certainly stand up to anything if, together with my sisters across Africa, we can educate more women! Education paves the way for more women leaders.

Fiona Mavhinga, lawyer and founding member of the CAMFED Association, the pan-African network of young women leaders for girls' education

Chapter 7

Misogyny and violence

Jess Hill

I want to start with a riddle.

There is a famous quote from the author Margaret Atwood that goes, 'Men are afraid that women will laugh at them. Women are afraid that men will kill them.'

Atwood's basis for writing this was not scientific. As she explains it:

> I asked some women students in a quickie poetry seminar I was giving, 'Why do women feel threatened by men?' 'They're afraid of being killed,' they said . . . 'Why do men feel threatened by women?' I asked a male friend of mine . . . 'They're afraid women will laugh at them,' he said. 'Undercut their world view.'[1]

From this straw poll came a conclusion with lyrical truth. When I was writing my book about domestic abuse, *See What You Made*

Me Do[2] – and as the #MeToo movement went viral – Atwood's line was invoked ad nauseum on social media. Women white-hot with anger over men's sexual violence held it aloft like a placard. *You think men have it hard? What pathetic little snowflakes!*

Atwood probably wasn't posing a riddle when she wrote those words, but I troubled over them like a homicide detective obsessing over a clue. On the face of it, Atwood was simply highlighting an absurd equivalence. It was easy (and, at the time of #MeToo, especially satisfying) to use it derisively. But turning her line over and over in my mind, I couldn't shake the feeling that there was more to it. That, somehow, these two fears were intrinsically connected. If men really did fear humiliation like women feared being murdered, what did that mean? Was humiliation – particularly at the hands of a woman – equated with a kind of obliteration for men? Why did the notion of being laughed at by a woman hold such power? Could getting to the bottom of this lead us closer to answering that $64 million question: *Why do men do it?*

•

When Julia Gillard delivered her misogyny speech in parliament in October 2012, I was a Middle East correspondent for *The Global Mail*, living in Beirut. I had never reported on gendered violence at that time and knew little then about the history of feminism and patriarchy. But as I watched the speech online, it was clear immediately that this was a historic moment. Gillard was saying the quiet bit – the unspeakable bit – out loud. The bit many women wouldn't even say among themselves. The bit that was *supposed* to remain unsaid.

You could measure the gravity of Gillard's transgression against the norm in the face of the opposition leader, Tony Abbott, as his default smirk dropped and the confident gleam left his eyes until his face was fixed in a grim rictus. His sleight-of-hand tactics were being exposed in front of him as nothing more than a sleazy old trick. Gillard was making the invisible visible.

It was the second time I had tuned in to Australian news in recent weeks. A fortnight earlier I had listened online, fists clenched and tears streaming, as ABC Radio Melbourne's morning broadcaster Jon Faine led a shattering program on the rape and murder of his colleague, Jill Meagher. This gorgeous woman who 'lit up a room' had simply been walking home after a night out with friends when she was *taken*. Her body discovered days later in a shallow grave. The grief and fury and goddamn helplessness of it all. Thousands would later march through the streets of Melbourne to remember Jill and other victims of men's violence. It was the start of something – a coming back to life for the women's movement, and a sign of much more to come.

As Jill's widower, Tom, would later reflect in a seminal essay on 'the monster myth', it was when he heard his wife's killer form a coherent sentence in court that he was able to truly grapple with the reality of men's violence against women. This was not simply the realm of psychopaths – of *monsters*. Violent men, he wrote, are socialised to objectify women, and they receive that messaging from the 'ingrained sexism and entrenched masculinity that permeates everything from our daily interactions all the way up to our highest institutions'. It was Jill, his 'favourite person', who had introduced him to these issues, 'before she was killed as a result of them'.[3]

By the time Meagher wrote those words in 2014, Tony Abbott had been elevated to the highest institution in the country. He had paid no real price for his craven misogyny, for standing in front of a sign that portrayed Australia's first female prime minister as a witch, for baiting pigheaded men in the media to taunt and objectify her. That reckoning would not come until many years later, in May 2022, when the government Abbott once led was shown at the ballot box that women would no longer tolerate their brazen contempt. There was, eventually, a price to pay for weaponising misogyny. As the saying goes, revenge is a dish best served cold.

In the decade since these two nation-changing events – the murder of Jill Meagher and Julia Gillard's misogyny speech – Australia's awareness of gendered violence has accelerated in a way no other country has matched. I think about those two watershed events now, realising I hadn't even made a connection between them. There was so little public understanding then about how violence and misogyny were connected; how the calculated deployment of sexism against a prime minister could form a dotted line to actual violence against women.

Those dots are connected more quickly now. We have had almost ten years of unswerving advocacy from stalwarts of the feminist movement, propelled to mainstream attention by the other-worldly grit and power of victim survivors such as Rosie Batty and, more recently, Grace Tame, among many others. It's not just gender studies students who see now how misogyny can be the propulsion fuel for men's violence against women; it's been established at the level of basic community awareness. As said the man who vanquished Abbott as prime minister, Malcolm Turnbull, 'Disrespecting women does not always result in violence against women. But all violence against women begins with disrespecting women.'[4]

We are now in the midst of a seismic shift, unprecedented in Western history. Victim survivors of sexual violence and abuse aren't just being heard – they're feted as icons. I was with Grace Tame on stage at the Adelaide Writers' Week in March 2022 and it felt more like a music festival. Thousands of people crammed onto every available patch of grass at Pioneer Gardens to hear Grace speak. Now, I'm not suggesting that we have banished the old era – in which victim survivors were pathologised, blamed, disregarded and disbelieved. Jurors remain so reluctant to believe rape victims that rape itself is all but decriminalised. But we *are* seeing a new era in which victim survivors (albeit still predominantly white, conventionally attractive and able-bodied victim survivors) are imbued with unique power, wisdom and expertise.

We're actually listening to victim survivors now; not just the blockbuster parts of their stories, but their whole stories. We're understanding how trauma works. We're finally grasping that the incident – the rape, the assault, the hit, the grope – is just the visible tip of a much greater iceberg. We know that some who go through the worst torture imaginable may never experience any physical violence. That some who are physically assaulted will say that it wasn't the worst part – or even that they are grateful to have marks on their bodies, because at least then they have proof of their abuse. That for others, it is the betrayal by institutions – the police, the family law system, their workplaces – that does more damage than anything their abuser ever did.

Finally, we are starting to see gendered violence not as a collection of physical incidents, but as a whole system of abuse. One that happens in private and in public. One that involves everyone from the perpetrator to the prime minister. We are finally – slowly – starting to shift our focus from the behaviour of victims to the actions of abusers; from the effect to the cause.

It may seem as though we've come a long way – and we have – but we cannot blink now. Unless we insist on an answer to the question of why men abuse, the cultural and psychological roots of sexism and misogyny will inevitably disappear once again from view, and we'll return to the tacit acceptance and normalisation of sexism that Gillard so stunningly highlighted in her speech to the national parliament.

I feel particularly attached to Australia's awakening to the realities of gendered violence, because it profoundly redirected the trajectory of my own life. In 2014, I had barely contemplated domestic abuse when I was asked to write a long feature article about it for *The Monthly*, a current-affairs journal based in Melbourne. That city was reeling once again after another homicide, this time of eleven-year-old Luke Batty, who was killed by his father, Greg Anderson, on a public cricket pitch. In the hours afterwards, from the depths of unimaginable pain and desolation, Luke's mother, Rosie, found something within herself that allowed her to stand before the cameras waiting outside her house. On that middle-class suburban street, armed with the colossal power of a mother's grief, Rosie shook the nation out of its slumber. On that day, Australians became *interested* in family violence. Suddenly, we needed to understand it, and we needed someone to explain why on earth, in the twenty-first century, it was still happening with such terrifying regularity.

If you're in any doubt about this regularity, consider this. In 1975, the first nationwide study of family violence was conducted in the United States. It found, much to the researchers' shock, that 28 per cent of married couples in America had experienced violence during their marriage. The conclusion those authors reached was stark: 'With the exception of the police and the military, the family is perhaps the most violent social group, and the home the most violent social setting, in our society.'[5] Today, that assessment stands. Despite everything we have done, the statistics have not changed.

When surveyed, one in four Australian women will say that, since the age of fifteen, they have been subjected to physical or sexual violence from an intimate partner. That's more than 2 million women.

We don't collect national statistics on violence against children, but smaller studies have shown it will affect around one in four. Around a million kids.

One in seven men will experience physical violence from a partner. That data is more complex to unpack: some will be physical aggression from a partner, but much of that violence will be from victims who are fighting back or defending themselves. That's 800,000 men.

All up, that's around 4 million Australians directly impacted by family violence in one way or another.

What about adults who grew up in an environment of family violence and coercive control? A nationwide British study showed that number to be one in five adults – if we use that figure, it gives us 4 million Australian adults whose life trajectories were significantly altered by the abuse they experienced in their formative years.

We don't count perpetrators. We can't even approximate their number. We can presume, however, that if many will victimise more than one partner or family member, it's not just one for one. So, let's say we have at least hundreds of thousands of perpetrators in Australia.

We can't just add all those numbers together and get a sum, because children who grow up with family violence have an increased likelihood of being victimised as adults or of ending up as perpetrators themselves.

But, at the very least, we're looking at four to five million Australians.

So, consider that line again: 'With the exception of the police and the military, the family is perhaps the most violent social group, and the home the most violent social setting, in our society.'

For many, that idea is almost impossible to absorb. Others know it in their bones.

When I sat down to write my first article about domestic abuse in 2014, I knew those statistics. I knew this was an important subject, and that I needed to do it justice. But, if I'm honest, I was weighed down by the same kneejerk tropes and stereotypes that had long kept this issue from being properly understood. Given 4500 words to *explain* it – not to interrogate a homicide, but to make sense of domestic violence as a social phenomenon – I didn't know where to start. I'm going to defame myself here and say that my thought process was something along the lines of, *How am I going to write 4500 words about a guy going home drunk on a Friday night and beating his wife?* I'm being unkind to make a point: in my mind, and in the minds of most Australians, domestic violence was defined predominantly as physical violence, along with a few other 'types' of abuse.

If it's any indication of how naive I was, a year into reporting on domestic abuse I wrote an article headlined 'Everything I thought I knew about domestic violence was wrong'.[6] Thanks largely to the victim survivors who educated me, I underwent a paradigm shift that would see me become obsessed with this subject for the next decade. Essentially, it became clear that we were largely looking at domestic abuse and family violence from the wrong end of the telescope. In focusing on the 'incidents' of abuse and violence, we were missing the bigger picture. In many of these cases, abuse was not something that happened at particular times – it was an unrelenting system, and the 'good times' were just as much a part of it as the 'bad'. In fact, the abuse itself was only a means to an end – and yet that end was something to which we were barely paying attention. That end goal, in so many cases, was control and entrapment. Abuse is the means; entrapment is the end.

What was also stunning to learn was that the majority of perpetrators follow a plotline that is so predictable that, once you know it, you can finish a victim's story before they're halfway through telling it. So predictable that when victim survivors get together, they marvel at the similarities in their experiences and say it's as though their perpetrators have all been studying from the same handbook.

Coercive control is the model for understanding what this typical plotline looks like. Victim survivors often say that when they hear coercive control explained, it's a light-bulb moment – especially for those who never thought of what they went through as domestic violence because they were never physically assaulted, or only rarely. In fact, most victims of coercive control do not even know they're being abused – even when they are subjected to physical and/or sexual violence – because they are made to believe that they are the crazy ones, and they are to blame.

The plotline looks different in every relationship but follows the same basic narrative structure. Coercive controllers isolate their victims from supportive friends and family; they deprive them of basic needs; they may constantly accuse them of infidelity and other betrayals to pressure them to prove their loyalty; they call and text relentlessly; they micromanage their victims' behaviour – setting rules about what they can wear, who they can see, what they should cook; they gaslight them, leading them to distrust their own minds; they monitor them through online communication tools or spyware; they intimidate and belittle them; they set rules intended to humiliate and degrade them, and establish clear consequences for breaking those rules; they may threaten the children, or enlist them as co-abusers; they may threaten or actually harm family pets; they destroy household goods; and they make it abundantly clear that if the victim leaves, there will be dire consequences – which may be veiled as a threat of self-harm. Sexual violence – both overt, and coercive – is common. Physical violence is common, but not necessary – the coercive controller only needs to establish the believable *threat* of violence to keep the system in place.

When you're trying to entrap your partner, there is perhaps nothing more effective than financial abuse, so it's unsurprising that this is almost universal in cases of coercive control. If your money is taken away from you, your dependence on your abusive partner is not just psychological but materially real. Research has shown there are common themes in financial abuse: interfering with women's employment; preventing women from having money; refusing to contribute to household bills; and creating debt for which women are liable. There are of course numerous ways in which financial abuse occurs – particularly through deception and fraud. For many women, there is a clear choice: stay with a violent partner or risk living under the poverty line. Many who leave will end up becoming single mothers: recent research by Dr Anne Summers has revealed that around 60 per cent of single mothers in Australia experienced physical and/or sexual violence from a former partner, and up to 70 per cent were subjected to coercive control.[7]

Coercive control, like all forms of abuse, can happen to anyone, but it affects certain groups of people at far higher prevalence than others. The Australian Institute of Criminology found in 2020 that the rates of coercive control were highest for women identifying as Aboriginal or Torres Strait Islander, women who spoke a language other than English in the home and women with a long-term health condition who needed daily assistance.[8] I use binary pronouns for ease of reference, and because men's use of coercive control is the most dangerous and the most common form it takes. In heterosexual relationships, this is a gendered form of abuse. But coercive control exists in LGBTQI+ relationships, and it follows the same architecture. What we're dealing with here is a patriarchal dynamic in which one person feels entitled to take control over another and has power they can leverage over the other person.

The language of coercive control – and an increasing understanding of it within the community – is very recent. When I released my book, in June 2019, there was virtually no public understanding of coercive control. That was the status quo until February 2020, when a personal trainer in Brisbane, Rowan Baxter, murdered his ex-wife Hannah Clarke and their three children by dousing her car in petrol and setting it on fire while they were inside. This was one of the most shocking family homicides in Australian history, and even more so because, prior to murdering them, Baxter's abuse was not characterised by physical violence. It did, however, tick all the boxes for coercive control.

Since then, and thanks in large part to the advocacy of Hannah's parents, Sue and Lloyd Clarke, and many others, such as Nithya Reddy in New South Wales, coercive control is now a subject of intense public interest.

The need for a sophisticated response to coercive control is critical, because coercive controllers are skilled at grooming friends, family, police, lawyers and judges – especially when they want to make it look as if their victim is the *real* perpetrator. In this way, they are a unique kind of offender – as one American police officer memorably put it, 'I've never been convinced by a bank robber to arrest the clerk.' This is such a recurrent tactic that it has its own acronym: DARVO – deny the accusation, attack whoever is making it and reverse the status of victim and offender. That a manipulation such as this is so common as to require its own shorthand again reminds us how deeply ingrained, how normal, are the expressions of one person exerting power over another in interpersonal human relationships – in the home, in schools, in social venues and in workplaces.

Not before time, companies are also waking up to how they can be used by perpetrators, and how their products have been weaponised. The Commonwealth Bank was alerted by one customer that her ex-partner was using one-cent transactions to harass her, by putting abusive messages in the description field. When they used artificial intelligence to scan all their online transactions, they found 100,000 potentially abusive transactions had been made in the space of three months. Allianz Insurance, with the University of New South Wales, identified the seven most common ways by which insurance could be used in family violence, including perpetrators cancelling insurance without their partners' knowledge.[9] This is, for many, a whole new way of understanding one of the most corrosive and dangerous social issues of our time – and it is light-years ahead of how the community at large has traditionally thought about domestic abuse.

•

Once we can see that this abuse is not just bad behaviour, but a process of entrapment, we can do away with that boilerplate question: 'Why doesn't she just leave?' In its place we can ask a far more confounding question: 'Why does he do it?' Why do abusive men – many of whom are not monsters – behave so monstrously?

As a society, we seem to have landed on a simple explanation: they do it for power and control, they do it because of gender inequality, because of male privilege – because they feel entitled to it.

But does that really get to the heart of why so many men *need* to exert such a twisted brand of power and control in their relationships? Why they are prepared to ruin not just their partners' lives but their own, in order to maintain it?

When I first started interrogating this question, it helped me to understand some of the recurring patterns that show up most frequently in abusive men. This is not about reducing men to two-dimensional categories. It is, however, possible to identify broad characteristics that commonly show up in men who use coercive control.

The first (and least prevalent) is the calculating abuser who knowingly manipulates and degrades his partner so that he can dominate her. These men actually *choose* a woman they think they can control. They are very attached to having someone to exert power over, but are typically not emotionally attached to that woman in particular. These men are more likely to have antisocial personality disorders, such as psychopathy and sociopathy.

Then there's the other pattern: the paranoid, insecure abuser who becomes more controlling over time because he's afraid his partner will leave and believes that they will hook up with someone else. Often jealous to the point of obsession, such men are prone to converting the most unlikely clues into evidence of betrayal.

There is so much more to say about other influences on why men become abusive, among them childhood and intergenerational trauma, mental illness and substance abuse. But while these individual life histories are important when it comes to designing interventions, our understanding of why abusive behaviour continues to proliferate can start from a place that's more universal, and tied to the way *all* boys and men are socialised.

Two factors seem to unite men who use coercive control: an overblown sense of entitlement and a radioactive victim complex. When these men feel thwarted – when they feel challenged or forced to compromise, for example – they can be triggered into a kind of humiliated fury.

Humiliated fury is essentially a cocktail of shame, rage and entitlement. As an emotional state, it performs a key function: it's a protective shield against feeling powerless and defective. By blaming others, or by abusing, controlling and oppressing them, one can regain a sense of power and avoid unbearable feelings of shame or vulnerability.

The emotional state of humiliated fury is particularly common to people whose identities are shaped by deep-seated (and often unacknowledged) feelings of shame. When shame is central to our identity, it can create terrible distortions in the way we perceive the things other people say or do. We may hear contempt in a voice that simply asks for compromise, or imagine disrespect where none was intended. When you feel inherently unlovable, worthless or damaged, it can become almost impossible to tell the difference between your own insecurities and the way others feel about you. So, shame-based people will see themselves as 'objects of derision'.

It was through interrogating the nexus of shame, fury and violence that I started to make sense of Atwood's line: that men's greatest fear is that women will laugh at them.

In fact, abusive men commonly see themselves as victims, convinced that their partners have shamed or disrespected them, however ridiculous and inaccurate that may be. It is from this position – of being attacked, disrespected, humiliated – that the abusive man believes he has a right to strike back. To protect himself, he will either strike back in the moment of perceived humiliation, or devise an ever-tighter regime of control and degradation to stop his partner from humiliating or disrespecting him again. As Germaine Greer notes in her essay *On Rage*, 'A red-blooded man is not supposed to take insult and humiliation lying down. He should not let people get away with doing things he thinks wicked or unjust. He demands the right both to judge and to act upon his judgment.'[10]

I think the psychoanalyst Erich Fromm gets close to the heart of what drives coercive control. 'The passion to have absolute and unrestricted control over a living being,' he writes, 'is the transformation of impotence into omnipotence.'[11]

Humiliated fury comes up again and again in stories of abusive men. I'm the real victim here. I could have been somebody. *They* stole it from me. *She* stole it from me. If she'd just been loyal, if she'd just listened, if she'd just done what I needed her to do – none of this would have happened. *See what she made me do?*

So why aren't we investigating, as a matter of urgency, what it is that's making hundreds of thousands of men in Australia feel such a shaky sense of self-worth, so impotent, *and* so entitled? Why is it they feel such existential terror at the notion of being humiliated? And, underpinning all of this, why is the culture of misogyny and contempt for women so resilient, even in the face of increased gender equality?

It goes back, according to the renowned family therapist Terry Real, to the contempt boys are taught to have for the so-called 'female' parts of themselves. Contempt, as he describes it, precedes all forms of violence, and is central to family violence and coercive control. 'First, you have to hold the victim as inferior to you and you as superior in some way, or you won't be able to victimise them,' he says. On the flip side of that is grandiosity. 'If you are talking about somebody who is violent or offensive, you are, by definition, talking about somebody who is in a state of grandiosity. They are superior, they are above you, they are above the rules. They are either holding the rules and/or you in contempt.'

Real says that this journey into contempt is a form of trauma in itself – a 'normal traumatisation' experienced by *all* boys when they learn that it's not safe to be emotional, expressive, vulnerable – anything 'girly'. That wound, Terry says, starts to occur in boys when they're very young – around three or four years old. 'Before our boys have learned to read, they have already read the code of masculinity. And there's research that indicates that boys are less expressive at three, four, five; it doesn't mean they *feel* less, but they've already figured out it's not politic to let people know what you feel. Three, four or five. That's a hell of a trauma.' What Real is describing here is the creation of a binary; or, as another family therapist, Olga Silverstein, called it, the 'halving' process. 'You take one whole human being, and you split them in half,' says Real. 'All the qualities to the left are feminine, all the qualities to the right are masculine. Traditionally the masculine is exalted, and the feminine is devalued. The essential relationship between masculine and feminine in Western culture is contempt. The masculine holds the feminine in contempt. What it means to be a man is to not be a woman in any way, shape, or form.'[12] Furthermore, the pressure to conform to this patriarchal standard of masculinity can be uncompromising: boys and men face harassment, exile and violence, particularly from other men, when they do not conform.

Boys who take the path of least resistance in our culture – who abide by our unspoken gender rules – have little choice but to betray their own hearts, and many can feel as though they need to wear a mask. To meet the standards of patriarchal masculinity, and to protect themselves against humiliation and even violence, they must hide intrinsic 'feminine' qualities within themselves. If they can't be true to their emotional selves, and particularly if they experience shaming or rejection from a parent, they may grow up hypersensitive to the threat of being exposed. They can harbour a terror that someone – especially an intimate partner, and/or their children – will see them as they see themselves: defective, vulnerable and unlovable. This is the shame and insecurity that underlies patriarchal masculinity. Is it any wonder that interpersonal violence persists at endemic levels – particularly against women? As the American psychologist Niobe Way puts it, 'If you raise boys to go against their nature, some of them will grow up and act crazy.'[13]

So, why does that Atwood quote tell us so much about the nature of gendered violence?

Of all the people I asked about this – about why women's derision posed such an existential threat to men – Real had the most concise response. 'Men are afraid of being laughed at, women are afraid of being killed,' he mused. 'The immediate thought, of course, is they're linked. Women will be killed if men are laughed at.'

'In order for a man to attack, there must be two things: there must be the wound, and there must be the entitlement to grandiosity,' he says. 'By going from shame to grandiosity, you can move from impotence to power over. And what's devilish about grandiosity is it feels good. It works. It pulls you out of the depression of your helplessness and you feel pumped. But it creates havoc in your world.

'Now, you may think that his feelings are – except that they're lethal – laughable. But men are fragile creatures, because traditional masculinity has no place for healthy self-esteem. Self-esteem comes from the inside out. And instead of healthy self-esteem, which comes from the inside out, 999 out of 1000 men replace it with performance-based esteem. I have worth because of what I can do. And that means that I'm only as good as my last game. And there's always somebody younger, faster, warming up in the bullpen,' says Real.[14] At the heart of men's use of violence is, essentially, fear.

To this day, our society provides cover for men who use humiliated fury to avoid responsibility. Laws of provocation, which still exist at least partially in some Australian jurisdictions, have in the past exempted men from murder convictions on the basis that, facing humiliation, they could not control themselves. In 2005, for example, Damian Sebo argued that he had been 'provoked' by his ex-fiancé, sixteen-year-old Taryn Hunt, who laughed at him, taunted him about his sexual performance and said he wouldn't have the guts to kill her. He bashed her so severely with a steering-wheel lock that he shattered her skull, and she died in hospital two days later. Using the defence of 'provocation', Sebo was acquitted of murder and convicted instead for manslaughter, with a minimum eight-year sentence. The message sent by the state is that when this teenage girl laughed at this man, he could not be expected to control his fury.

We cannot pretend that domestic abuse, rape, sexual harassment and child sexual abuse occur in a vacuum. There's an epidemic of violence against women in this country, and to confront it we can't just focus on gender inequality. We need to define and discuss the system that entraps *both* sexes, because domestic abuse doesn't really start with men disrespecting women. Its roots go much deeper – into men's fear of other men, and into the way patriarchy shames them into rejecting their own so-called 'feminine' traits such as empathy, compassion, intuition and emotional intelligence. We need to talk about how, for too many men, patriarchy makes power a zero-sum game and shrinks the rich landscape of intimacy to a staging ground for competition and threat. This is the realm of men's violence, with its underworld of misogyny, contempt, shame – and humiliated fury.

A friend forwarded the speech to me. You've got to watch this, she said. Oh, sure, I thought. I lived in Canberra, went to parliament now and then, and thought nothing authentic would ever be spoken there.

I watched with a raw, electric exhilaration that was also fear. Would she lose her nerve? Would she be howled down? Could she – could any woman – get away with delivering the truth right into the smirking faces of those who'd always silenced us? In those fifteen minutes of exquisitely controlled, steely rage and sustained, authoritative eloquence, Julia Gillard showed us the way.

Kate Grenville, Australian author

I was on a holiday in Greece, sailing, with a poor signal. My friend Cathy Hunt, who built the WOW – Women of the World Festivals in Australia, rang. Seemingly breathless with amazement and excitement, she was saying something that I couldn't quite hear about Julia Gillard and 'misogyny' and 'nailing it' and 'nothing like it *ever*'. Knowing the torrent of focused male viciousness that had emanated from Julia's opponents from when she first held power, I thought they had made a further malign move to humiliate and damage her. But no! When I reached land and saw the Shakespearian magnificence of her retaliation I was jubilant. Yes, she'd nailed it. Yes, she'd outed the true nature of the beast. And yes, we all basked in her glory and signed up for her call to arms.

Jude Kelly CBE, CEO and founder of
The WOW Foundation and WOW Festivals

Chapter 8

Misogyny in politics: 'There's just something about her'

Jennifer Palmieri

I did not have the courage to speak to Hillary that night.

Time seemed to be moving at a different velocity, and even in the moment it was hard for me to keep track of the clock. But my best recollection of events is that it was around 8.30 pm when our campaign manager pulled me out of the hotel conference room we were using to track election returns and told me that we had a problem. He said the votes for Hillary were coming in about two to four percentage points below what our internal polls had predicted. He did not say outright that he thought we would lose. I don't think he could permit himself to form those words in his head, let alone have them come out of his mouth. I certainly was not ready to hear them. Instead, he asked me if I had any advice for how he should present this news to Hillary, and if I wanted to come with him to tell her.

My answer to both questions was 'no'. As campaign communications director, I was on the road with Hillary every day and had been the one to deliver a lot of bad news to her, including the critical development in the closing days before the election that FBI Director James Comey had reopened his investigation of her email practices when she was Secretary of State. This time, I could not do it. The thought of having to watch her face as she absorbed the news that she would lose – after all she had been through during that gruelling campaign and all that was on the line for the nation – was unbearable. I also feared what I imagined would be a look of reprimand in her eyes. *I told you so.*

Despite what the polls had predicted, I knew Hillary would be the least surprised out of anyone on the campaign that we had lost. The truth is that, although she had been widely expected to run for president in 2016, she joined the race with some reluctance, in part because she understood how hard it would be for a woman to win. Throughout both the contentious Democratic primary and the general election, she expressed unease that our campaign was not meeting the moment when it came to dealing with voters' frustrations and combatting the relentless attacks coming her way. We all told her repeatedly it would be fine.

I don't feel as if we failed her so much as we kidded ourselves into thinking all the difficulties we faced – from Donald Trump's misogynist attacks and nasty 'Lock her up' rallies, to Russian-orchestrated leaks of our campaign emails, to an FBI investigation into Hillary's past actions – were manageable. She could feel what was happening, all the forces – seen and unseen, cosmic and earthly – that were lining up against her. Intellectually, I understood that it was possible we could lose. Our own campaign polling showed a one in four chance of losing the election. Nevertheless, in my heart, I did not believe a loss to be possible. It would be too unfair, too counter to what I thought I knew of American values, for Donald Trump to win over Hillary Clinton.

But all actions in the universe have a reaction, and Trump's victory provoked an immediate, ferocious backlash among women in the United States. Trump was never popular with women, but the grossly misogynistic behaviour displayed on the 'Access Hollywood tape' brought him to a new low, causing him to lose support even among some Republican women.[1] The behind-the-scenes footage, released in early October 2016, showed Trump, then a newly married man, speaking crudely of how his wealth and power gave him the ability to do whatever he wanted to women, including grabbing them by their genitals. The release of the video prompted more than a dozen women to come forward to allege that Trump had sexually harassed or assaulted them in the past.[2] Billy Bush, the former Access Hollywood anchor caught snickering along with Trump in the video, lost his job. Donald Trump was elected President of the United States.

Women were enraged. They took to the streets on the day after Trump's inauguration by the millions as part of the 2017 Women's March. While the numbers of people protesting across the country were huge, the march effort was criticised by some for having no policy agenda, and by others for having too radical an agenda. But I knew those political characterisations of the event missed the point. The people marching were simply furious, and they wanted the world to know it. The palpable rage and sense of empowerment on display that day did not end there.

The energy of the Women's March fed into the Me Too movement, in which women who had been sexually assaulted and harassed by men sparked a revolution of accountability. Women made gains in politics as well. In 2018, a record number of women ran for elected office, and they won in historic numbers as well. The number of women in Congress grew by more than a third, jumping from 89 women elected in 2016 to 117 in 2018. A woman was sworn in as Speaker of the House of Representatives for the first time.[3] Sixteen women ran for state governors in 2018 and nine of them won, matching the record high for female governors across the country. In 2020, the number of women in Congress grew again to a record high of 120, making up 27 per cent of Congress.[4] And nearly a third of America's biggest cities are now led by female mayors.[5]

Hillary was lionised, too, during the Trump years, as the prescient martyr the world should have listened to and elected. It was nice to see her lauded, but the appreciation of her after the fact felt hollow. It concerned me that the backlash to Trump's election seemed to manifest more in outrage that the misogynist Trump had won than in any appreciation of the role misogyny towards Hillary had played in her loss. The fact that women holding elected office in the United States is at a record high and, at the same time, still pitifully low, speaks to the degree of ingrained misogyny in America's political power systems.

The failure of America to elect a female president also stands as a glaring tribute to the difficulties women face. Six women ran for the Democratic nomination in the 2020 presidential campaign. Despite the conventional wisdom among political press going into the 2020 Democratic primary that it would be a tough cycle for white male candidates, given the gains women had made in 2018, the primary started and ended with two white men in their seventies – Joe Biden and Bernie Sanders – leading in the polls. Rather than making an effort to battle the misogyny in the American electorate, Democrats considering who was the best candidate to take on Trump seemed to judge it more prudent to acquiesce to its presence.[6]

The day after Hillary's loss, I was already hearing Democrats say, 'Well, we can't do that again. Next time it will have to be a man.' This willingness to tolerate low-grade misogyny only helps to perpetuate it, and that is why it's so important to name all the ways misogyny hurt our campaign. This is not just about politics. Women in America and around the world face the same kind of discrimination that plagued Hillary – albeit on a less public stage – every single day.

Moreover, there is too much on the line to not continue the fight. The women's rights movement is a relatively new phenomenon in America. Consider this: Hillary Clinton's mother was born on the day Congress took the final action to give women the right to vote, in June 1919. In the span of Dorothy Rodham's lifetime, America went from women winning the right to vote to her daughter coming close to being the first woman to win a major party's nomination for President of the United States. Despite the recent electoral wins for women and the 2020 defeat of the misogynist Trump, the gains women have made over the past hundred years are in jeopardy. America seems to be undergoing a backlash to the backlash that is the fight for women's rights.

For example, more than a dozen states have recently acted to all but ban abortion outright.[7] Perversely, Justices of the Supreme Court have argued that the right to an abortion does not exist because it was not conferred in the original Constitution, ignoring the fact that women weren't mentioned in that document at all. The founding documents of the United States – both the Declaration of Independence and the Constitution – were written by white men, and excluded women and all people of colour from the start.

Women and other marginalised populations in America are still struggling to recover from injustices – most notably slavery – made at the creation of this country. All of this is happening against the backdrop of America's changing demographics, in which the number of white Americans is decreasing and, while they continue to hold the vast majority of positions of power, the numbers of white men are dwindling. It feels like a race against the clock. More Americans are aware of racism and misogyny than ever before, but the question remains, are both racism and misogyny so built into America's power systems and psyche that it is too late to rid ourselves of them?

Misogyny must be named to be understood, deconstructed and left in the past. None of us here today created this world where biases about women, particularly women in power, persist. Most of us – women and men alike – are trying to sort it all out and move forward. But there remains something that makes us uneasy about the women leading the forward movement. They continue to draw fire.

When I first joined the Clinton campaign in the spring of 2015, I was fairly naive to the challenges Hillary was to face. I did not think it was going to be hard or even that significant for America to elect its first woman president. We had already elected our first Black president. Given the history of slavery and racial discrimination in America, electing the first woman seemed a comparatively easy task. Also, thanks in part to the work Hillary had done in her 2008 presidential campaign, Americans no longer questioned whether a woman could do the job of president. Early polls from 2016 not only showed that voters were comfortable with a woman in that role, but also that Clinton entered the race as the clear frontrunner to win both the Democratic nomination and the general election. At the time, I didn't see how America could both believe the woman was going to win and view her through a misogynistic lens.

While I did not see the difficulties the first woman to be nominated for president by a major US political party would face, as I noted earlier, Hillary did try to warn me. On my first day on the campaign staff, she sat me down and basically vomited up a summary of what it had been like to be her for the prior three decades. She wanted me to hear it all so I had an inkling of what the campaign was likely to encounter in representing her to the press and the public.

Hillary held forth for more than an hour, starting with her husband's campaigns for Governor of Arkansas and her belated decision to change her name to 'Clinton' after voters expressed disapproval of her continuing to use the name 'Rodham'. Next, she recounted the turmoil of the White House years and the backlash she experienced when, as First Lady, she took on the controversial issue of healthcare reform, while – surprisingly – the public came to her side and supported her in big numbers when it was revealed her husband had been unfaithful to her.[8]

Finally, she walked through challenges that had arisen in her own campaigns. Hillary began with describing the work that had been required to win over women voters in her 2000 New York Senate race who were distrustful of her decision to remain with her husband after his infidelity. During the 2008 Democratic presidential primary campaign, voters had to be convinced Hillary was tough enough to be commander-in-chief. The team made this effort a major focus of her 2008 campaign and its work paid off. Eventually, Democratic voters were convinced that Hillary had the character and experience to do the job of president. Then, as

Hillary described it, the problem was that voters just didn't like her. The 2008 campaign was never able to put the two attributes together – to be seen as tough enough to be president but also likeable enough for people to want to vote for her. It was a struggle we would face in the 2016 race as well.

It is Hillary's practice to thoughtfully consider criticism of her to see if she can learn from it, but after many tumultuous decades in public life, it had become nearly impossible to disentangle legitimate critiques from the sexism that was clearly at play. She did not offer any direction to me about what I was to do about all of this, except to say I should be aware of the history and know that – while I should never censor myself when it came to telling her how I thought we should manage the press – she was likely to be sceptical as to whether much would improve in this realm. She concluded by saying that she saw herself as 'just a simple and serious person', and was baffled that she provoked such rage from some quarters.

I laughed at her description of herself as a 'simple and serious person', because on top of that she is a warm, fun, reliable friend who is also brilliant. She is not 'just' a simple and serious person, but I knew what she meant. She is 'simple' in that she is direct. She doesn't have a lot of time for pretence. (For all the grief Hillary gets for being inauthentic, the truth is that she is terrible at 'faking it' and bearing dumb or sexist questions the way other women leaders can). She is 'serious' in that she really worries about the state of the world and wants to solve problems, not just look as if she is trying to solve them. These are qualities we should seek in a president.

Listening to 'simple and serious' Hillary was a poignant moment, too. I saw a human being, who happens to be named 'Hillary Clinton', who was as bewildered as anyone else by the phenomenon that is 'Hillary Clinton'. She seemed to me to be as uneasy with some of the adulation that is thrown her way as she is with the attacks. Neither reflects an understanding of the person she really is.

Eighteen months later – standing in a ballroom of the New Yorker Hotel on the afternoon of Wednesday 9 November, nodding and smiling as supporters of Hillary lauded her very gracious concession speech – I finally got it. 'Where was "this Hillary" during the campaign?' friends of hers, both men and women, lamented. 'Why didn't we see this side of her when it mattered?'

Yes, I am sure you loved her concession speech, I thought. *Because that's what you think is acceptable for a woman to do – concede.*

I then understood why we liked 'this Hillary' so much better than 'candidate Hillary'. Fundamentally, it wasn't about the words she used in her concession speech. It wasn't even about her. It was what she represented. Hillary was no longer radical change personified – a woman pushing to be President of the United States. She was a gracious loser putting the needs of her country above her own. That is a role we are comfortable seeing a woman play. It was the role of Hillary as an ambitious candidate that troubled us.

It was a paradox of the campaign that Hillary Clinton's eminent standing as a member of the Democratic establishment obscured the fact that she was also a groundbreaking pioneer who defined new roles for women. Since Hillary delivered her student commencement speech at Wellesley College and landed on the cover of *Life* magazine as the female face of the baby boomers in 1969, she was a challenging figure of her generation. She was the 'lady lawyer' married to the Governor, who hadn't taken her husband's name and made more money than he did. Next, she was the first wife of a major presidential candidate who had her own career and didn't 'stay home to bake cookies', as she famously said, to much criticism, during her husband's 1992 presidential campaign. She was the first First Lady who worked in the West Wing and took on the touchiest of touchy political issues, health care. She was the first First Lady to run for Senate, to run for president, to become Secretary of State and to run for president again.

As someone who was constantly stepping outside the confines of the box in which women had traditionally been put, Hillary was always confounding the public (as the ups and downs in her approval ratings demonstrate). There is no model to compare her to; she doesn't make sense to us. 'There is just something about her I don't like.' This, and its sister complaint, 'There's just something about her I don't trust,' was so often heard that we developed an acronym for it: TJSAH. It would come up in focus groups with voters time and again. The facilitators would push participants to be specific about what they did not like, but their answers were perpetually vague – along the lines of 'She's hiding something' or 'She's always so sketchy.' It is a critique you hear said about powerful women across the board, in and outside of politics. And it's this sentiment, where a person would feel an underlying, but unspecific, suspicion of Hillary Clinton, that led voters to conclude – as we often heard – they were 'fine with a woman being president, just not *this* woman.'

Seen through today's modern lens, none of what Hillary has done, including running for president, may seem revolutionary. If we step back and look at it in the scope of human history, however, it is a radical and recent concept for a woman to be in charge. More than forty years after Hillary Clinton entered public life, there still isn't a model you can compare her to, and she still doesn't make sense to us. It is hard for people, women included, to relate to her.

I fear that our campaign strategy to elect the first woman president only served to compound the difficulty voters had in relating to her. In effect, we set out to prove that it *didn't matter* that Hillary Clinton was a woman. And we did. We showed that she could do the job of president as it had been done by every man before her – reducing her to a female facsimile of the qualities voters expect to see in a male president. This left her jammed into an ill-fitting role and robbed of some of her own unique qualities. In retrospect, it's no wonder many found her to be inauthentic.

It was this question of authenticity, and our collective unease with an ambitious woman, that were at the root of the most vexing issue of the 2016 campaign – Hillary's use of a private email account during her time as Secretary of State. In retrospect, particularly given the norm-busting that went on during the Trump presidency, Hillary's email practice was so insignificant a concern it would almost be comical had it not been so devastating.

The summer of 2015, when we were really drowning in the email controversy, saw the most difficult days of the whole campaign. We were trying to decipher – and I use that word quite literally, as to us it was as unclear and confusing as if it were written in code – what was really behind the uproar the email story had caused, and what we could do to move beyond it. The press's goalposts for the questions Hillary needed to address were always moving. First, we had to establish that using a personal email account was legal. We established that. To this day, no one is satisfied with our answer. Next the press said, 'She needs to explain why she used a personal email account.' She explained. It was not good enough. 'No, tell us why she *really* did it,' they would say to me. Next, it was, 'She needs to admit it was a mistake.' She said it was a mistake. That wasn't good enough either.

After many painful conversations on the matter, we finally decided in late August 2015 that Hillary should do a series of interviews where she could answer more questions about the emails, with the hope of putting the matter behind us once and for all. Per our earlier discussion, Hillary was sceptical that the interviews would help. She had already answered dozens of questions about her emails, to no effect, but she agreed, reluctantly, to proceed with the plan.

She did an interview in which she said it had been a mistake to use a personal email account. The interviewer then asked if Hillary owed the American people an apology. *An apology to the American people?* I thought. *For what?*

In all the hours of torturous discussions we had, painstakingly going over every question that could possibly arise in any interview, the question of whether she needed to apologise had not occurred to us. Whatever harm had come from the issue of the emails, Hillary – and not the American people – had borne the brunt of it. Still, my heart sank when I heard the question. I knew once the spectre of an apology had been raised, the press would never move on until she gave one. Again, Hillary was not happy about it, but she saw the same reality we all did and apologised in her next interview.

That's when it all became clear to me: *They don't want her to apologise. They want her to confess to a crime she didn't commit. There's nothing she can do. It will* never *be enough.*

What the email controversy revealed was an age-old suspicion surrounding women – going back to the days of witchcraft trials and before. If it wasn't her emails, it would have been something else: another issue, equally trivial and irrelevant, for which Hillary would have been tortured. Because underneath all the never-ending series of questions about emails lay the fundamental truth that what all of this was really about was that there was just something about Hillary Clinton – an intelligent, capable, ambitious woman in a position of power – that made voters and the press uncomfortable.

To try to better understand the gender dynamics at play in the campaign, we sought the advice of social researchers and even psychologists. These researchers do important work trying to uncover what is behind the attacks that are directed at powerful women in all sectors, and they offered advice about ways we could try to work around the gender bias. For example, we were advised that we needed to put a lot of effort into explaining Hillary's motivations for wanting to be in politics, as it was at odds with the traditional view of woman as communal and nurturing. The solution, we were told, was to express Hillary's motivation for running for president as a desire to be 'in service to others'.

To prove her motivations were rooted in wanting to do good in the world (and not in seeking to promote herself), she talked about her mother's difficult childhood, and why it propelled her to choose public service as a career and to work with the Children's Defense Fund. We were also told that Hillary's most popular attribute with voters was that she had been willing to go to work for President Obama, the man she had lost to in the 2008 presidential primary, as his Secretary of State. To them, it was evidence that she really was willing to put being 'in service to others' above her own ambition to be president. It was tough to make people feel comfortable with Hillary's ambition, so I was grateful we had hit upon an attribute of hers that voters embraced. Still, I found it disconcerting that people didn't appreciate the outstanding job she had done as Secretary of State so much as they approved of her going to work for the man who had defeated her.

Finally, we were advised how to best address the unique concerns some women voters had regarding female candidates. These women voters wanted to know that the female candidate had more experience than they did – so they had confidence she could do the job – but not so much more experience that they felt inferior to the candidate. It was not a needle we were able to thread. Our failure to strike this balance played out in focus groups with women voters, who would point to Hillary's extraordinary accomplishments as something that alienated, rather than impressed, them. They could not relate to her. Talk about a no-win scenario – where will we find a qualified female candidate for president who is a relatable figure for women who have been prevented from following their own ambitions?

Gender bias and the questions it raises – about a woman's ambitions, her qualifications, her likeability – continue to vex women candidates today. In 2021 and 2022, the Barbara Lee Family Foundation (BLFF), an organisation that conducts research on gender bias in politics, conducted in-depth polling and focus groups to determine how American voters were feeling about women candidates and, because so many women had been elected in 2018, women incumbent leaders.[9] The research showed that, first, voters in America continue to question women's qualifications for office, relative to men – they assume men are qualified for office, while women have to prove it; second, voters are inclined to believe that a woman leader has not been effective unless she constantly reminds them of her qualifications for the job and what she has accomplished in it; and, third, it is non-negotiable with voters that women have to be likeable, but also tough enough to do the job.

It's not all bleak news, though. The research also showed that a majority of voters are concerned that women face unfair sexism when running for office and, in a distinct change from what research showed in 2016, voters believe women should call out sexist attacks when they happen, lest they go unaddressed and self-perpetuate. It's frustrating that these obstacles continue to exist, but it's good news that voters are more aware of the way gender bias hurts women leaders and want it to end.

Consistent with the obstacles identified in the BLFF research, the 2020 Democratic Party presidential primary was another window into the maddeningly persistent ways in which we're conditioned to see men as leaders, and are still uneasy with – or, worse, uninterested in – women with presidential ambitions. Unlike the 2016 campaign, where Hillary entered the race as the frontrunner and was the subject of intense press interest and scrutiny, the six women running for the Democratic nomination struggled to break through at all.

White men consistently topped the early polls, and when voting started in early 2020, only white men – former mayor of South Bend, Indiana, Pete Buttigieg, Senator Bernie Sanders and Joe Biden – won any of the state primary elections. The women had been unable to gain traction in the polls even though none of them had ever lost an election before, and most had significantly more governing experience than some of the men running, particularly the relatively young Buttigieg. Then-Senator Kamala Harris had held statewide office since 2010 and had won three state elections in California; more than 5 million people cast a vote for her in the 2016 Senate elections. Senators Kirsten Gillibrand and Amy Klobuchar were in their third Senate terms, and Elizabeth Warren was in her second term as Senator. In contrast, Buttigieg never held statewide office, and the city he represented as mayor was significantly smaller than a Congressional district, while both Biden and Sanders had previously run in and failed to win presidential primaries.

For a time, in the fall of 2019, Senator Elizabeth Warren was at the top of the pack. She led national polls and money was rolling in to her campaign. Her success also meant she was coming under attack, the most potent of which focused on the vagueness of her proposals around health care. She answered those criticisms with a new healthcare plan and details of how she would pay for it. From that point on, she dropped in the polls and never fully regained her footing. Many pointed to that moment as the beginning of the end for her campaign, saying the healthcare plan put her at odds with both progressives and moderates within the Democratic Party, but I see other forces at play here.[10]

We are comfortable with women as leaders in abstract, but when they get close to gaining real power – as Warren did when she approached the frontrunning position – we get uneasy, and start questioning them and their motivations in a way we do not question male candidates. Bernie Sanders did not have a good answer for how he would pay for his healthcare policies, but questions about his plan didn't hinder and plague him the way they hurt Warren. Again, voters had no problem with a woman candidate; they just couldn't get behind *this* woman, who inspired suspicion in a way that, incidentally, a male candidate did not. Or, as one writer for the humour website McSweeney's Internet Tendency aptly put it shortly after Senator Warren joined the 2020 race, 'I don't hate women candidates – I just hated Hillary and coincidentally I'm starting to hate Elizabeth Warren.'[11]

Warren did not make her job easier by adopting 'big structural change' as her rallying cry. That can be scary for voters coming from any candidate, man or woman. During the campaign Warren was famous for having a policy plan for everything, but, tellingly, her stump speech did not focus on policy.[12] Instead, she spent most of her speech telling us about herself and making us feel comfortable with this ambitious woman who wanted to change so much.

Lest we think she was pursuing a lifelong dream to be the first woman president, in her stump speech she assured voters, 'I have already had my dream job; it was to be a special education teacher.' The first time I heard her say this, I had to stop myself from gasping in admiration. Knowing how uneasy voters can be when it comes to ambitious women, she presented her ambition as being *in the past*. Also, her dream job was tied to a traditional, non-threatening role for women: being a teacher. Understanding that she must also be likeable, Warren was relentlessly joyful on the trail. She greeted questions from voters with an expectant smile on her face, reminiscent of every teacher we ever loved growing up. Even though I could recite each word of her stump by heart, watching her deliver the speech would mesmerise me every time. She was that effective a communicator.

Still, my heart sank as I watched what she had to do. So much time and effort was spent trying to make voters comfortable with her, while, outside the confines of whatever room she was speaking in, larger forces in the primary swirled about, with Democrats eventually selecting Joe Biden – as polls from 2017 onwards had always said they would – as their best choice to take on Trump.

Despite her best efforts, Warren failed. Likewise, none of the steps we took on the Clinton campaign assuaged voters' concerns about Hillary's ambition. Ultimately, there really is no way around it; we must plough through the consternation by pushing back against the double standard until such time when a woman declaring her ambition to the world is celebrated as much as when a man does it. Because we cannot allow another generation of women to feel fear about expressing their ambition, or spend another election cycle shadow-boxing with ourselves about whether a woman candidate is 'electable'. We must dismantle these old power structures by dismantling what's in our own heads. As Senator Amy Klobuchar is fond of saying, the obstacles are the path and they will show us the way.

•

I am grateful to have been spared the memory of whatever expression was on Hillary's face when she understood she was going to lose. By the time I saw her the next day, at the concession speech, she wore a countenance of steely determination. It helped her to get through the day.

But the cowardice I exhibited that election night continued to bother me. So, in the fall of 2017, I asked Hillary if I could come to see her and get some things off my chest. She had been right, all along, about how hard it was going to be to elect the first woman. She alone saw it all happening in real time, and I was desperately sorry that we could not do more to combat all the attacks that came her way.

There was no look of reprimand in her eyes when I said all of this to her. Rather, she told me that by the time we got to the end of the campaign, she, too, expected to win. I remember seeing her on the Monday night before the election. We held huge election-eve rallies in Philadelphia, Pennsylvania, and Raleigh, North Carolina, with President Obama, Bruce Springsteen, Jon Bon Jovi and Lady Gaga. It felt victorious. I have a great photo someone took of her teasing me on our campaign plane as we were flying back from

North Carolina to New York. She looks happy. It's heartbreaking to have believed you were going to win and then lose. But this loss was always going to be heartbreaking. I am glad she at least had that one night – one night when a woman in America believed that she was going to be the next President of the United States.

Even after all I have seen, I still think we are on the path to electing the first woman president. However, it will only happen if men and women in America commit not just to being concerned about the sexism women face, but seek to understand and combat the misogyny at the root of that sexism. I am optimistic because I have faith in the power of American women. They are not backing down. Plus, depending on how you keep score, a woman has already won an election for president. Hillary Clinton got close to 3 million more votes than Donald Trump. She proved it was possible.

Someday, America will have a woman president and I am fine with it. I just really wanted it to be this woman.

When Julia delivered her powerful parliamentary speech in 2012, it was quite a moment. Her direct, forceful rebuke of misogyny in the halls of the government she led was brave, moving and echoed not only throughout Australia but the world. She reminded us that in order to fight for progress we must directly reject those who want to see us go backwards, and she did so with her signature grit and grace. Ten years later, it remains a poignant reminder of how far we've come, and how far we still have to go.

Hillary Clinton, former US Secretary of State, US Senator and 2016 Democratic Presidential Nominee

It's hard to believe it's been ten years since Julia delivered the famous misogyny speech. Though much progress has been made towards gender equity since then, many issues remain unresolved. The misogyny speech is one that speaks truth to power, challenging the entrenched prejudices that women face daily. The female leaders we interviewed for our book *Women and Leadership: Real lives, real lessons* constantly found themselves being judged on their appearance and not on substance.

The misogyny speech is fierce and unapologetic. Julia stands up for women, young and old, calling out sexism, disrespect, misogyny and prejudice. She demands that misogynists take responsibility for their words and actions, particularly when they are in positions of power. Ten years on, this speech still resonates; it is my hope that ten years from now it will no longer resound with so many.

Ngozi Okonjo-Iweala, Director-General of the World Trade Organization, the first woman and the first African to serve in that role, and former Finance Minister of Nigeria, the first woman to serve in that role

Chapter 9

Misogyny in today's world of work

Rosie Campbell

Sexism has never rendered women powerless. It has either suppressed their strength or exploited it.

bell hooks[1]

Women's presence in the workplace isn't new. Women have always contributed to economic life through, for example, 'gathering', subsistence farming or weaving. As modern work evolved, women were employed in factories, in hospitals and in myriad industries as secretaries and largely lower-ranking administrators. Crucially, however, women's talents were frequently suppressed, or exploited, ensuring that only privileged men accrued the most lucrative rewards of paid work, and only men could reach the upper ranks of hierarchies, occupy professional fields and be highly financially remunerated. Of course, this exploitation was not limited only to women; privileged men's advantage was sustained by structures of class and race as well as gender. While much has changed in the modern world of work, persistent inequalities between genders, intersected by race and class, continue to shape people's experiences of paid employment, and these inequalities are sustained, at least in part, by misogyny and certainly by sexism.

Sexism and misogyny are related but distinct attitudes. Misogyny refers to fear of, hatred of or entrenched prejudice against women, while sexism manifests in 'systematic discrimination, or failure to take women into account'.[2] Misogyny and sexism can be both externalised and internalised: internalised misogyny is when women project misogynistic attitudes on to other women and even on to themselves. Both forms have a destructive impact on individual and collective experiences of the workplace, and both lead to the devaluing of women's work and the exploitation of their labour.

In discussing misogyny and sexism in the world of work, we need to recognise that contemporary workplaces are gendered.[3] Formal, paid employment is characterised by horizontal gender segregation – that is, the under-representation or over-representation of women and men in certain occupations or industries – and vertical gender segregation – the imbalance between the numbers of men and women in leadership roles. The hierarchical structure of the world of work creates environments where power typically skews towards men, who occupy the upper echelons of organisations and a disproportionate number of prestigious, high-profile and well-paid positions. According to *Fortune*, women run just 41 of the 500 largest companies in the world.[4] Despite some progress, women are still over-represented in low-paid and insecure positions.[5] Women are more often employed in caring and service-sector roles, and men in industry and finance.[6] Even in sectors where women form the majority of the workforce, men still dominate leadership positions; for example, globally women make up 70 per cent of healthcare workers but just 30 per cent of leadership positions in that industry.[7]

The pervasive cultures of misogyny and sexism that entrenched these gender divisions in the world of work have changed rapidly in many high-income countries, with the result that often the original sources of patriarchy have faded from the contemporary imagination. A snapshot of the opportunities available to men and women in middle-class jobs from the dominant ethnic group in wealthy nations leads a persistent minority of people to believe that sexism and misogyny have been eradicated from the workplace. An international survey conducted by the Global Institute for Women's Leadership (GIWL) with the polling company Ipsos in 2022 found that 18 per cent of respondents believed that gender inequality doesn't exist (21 per cent of men and 14 per cent of women).[8] If only that were so.

The modern gender division of labour at work has diverse historical roots shaped by the industrial revolution, colonisation and slavery. The industrial revolution led to a vast movement of work away from the home and local vicinity, and to the emergence of large employers.[9] The creation of factories and the like produced a greater gender segregation of work, with men more often undertaking paid employment and women more often performing unpaid domestic and caring work. Working-class women and women from marginalised groups continued to take on paid work outside of the home, but an aspirational gender-role ideology developed in the wake of the industrial revolution, along with the emergent middle class, that valorised the position of women within the home as unpaid carers. At the same time, the public sphere was conceptualised as an exclusively male space, and the ideal worker as a man unencumbered by domestic or caring responsibilities.

These gender-role ideologies underlie many stereotypes and norms about the appropriate behaviours and activities for women and men that endure to this day. Attitudes to gender roles have always varied across time and place but the modern period has seen a truly seismic shift, with a rapid expansion of opportunities for women and men to diverge from traditional expectations. However, in some contexts traditional outlooks persist, and the extent of the change varies by generation and across cultures.

In this chapter I mainly focus on the impact of misogyny and sexism on women undertaking paid employment in the formal economy. It should be acknowledged, however, that these attitudes perhaps have an even more profound impact on the experiences of women working in the informal economy. According to UN Women, the United Nations agency for gender equality, 740 million women across the world work in the informal economy.[10] Misogyny and sexism contribute to the difficulties many of those women experience in accessing the employment rights and relative financial security a formally recognised paid job can provide. Unequal access to education, intersecting inequalities, gendered assumptions regarding responsibility for domestic work and cultures that discourage public interaction with men all limit women's opportunities to gain formal employment. The precarity of much informal employment, the lack of legal protection and absence of human resources departments mean women employed outside the formal world of work are particularly vulnerable to abuses of power. Migrant women are often especially exposed.[11]

The relative lack of value that is placed on care work in modern society also has its roots in historic hierarchies of gender, race and class. In the post-Enlightenment period, from the late eighteenth century onwards, women were not only assigned to the so-called private sphere – at least in the wealthy classes and in the imagined ideal – but the domestic work in which they engaged was devalued and deemed not 'real work'.[12] The ongoing impact of this is reflected in the low pay and poor conditions experienced by those employed in care work (such as nursing, child care and elder care, and social work) and domestic work (such as in-home care, cleaning and gardening in private households) in many nations. The International Labour Organization (ILO) estimates that 63.5 per cent of paid care workers are women.[13] Domestic workers who are immigrant women are particularly vulnerable to sex-based harassment, violence and abuse, and are at risk of modern slavery.[14] The ILO estimates that 81 per cent of domestic workers are engaged in informal employment.[15] In many ways, the barriers to equality for these workers are even greater and require international action and coordination to overcome.

In the formal economy, women can be met with backlash from those resistant to change when they are seen to violate gender norms by entering male-dominated industries and workplaces. One form of backlash is sex-based harassment – that is, 'behavior that derogates, demeans, or humiliates an individual based on that individual's sex' and is rooted in intersecting forms of discrimination.[16,17] Research has shown that sex-based harassment is employed as a means of exerting power and control, attempting to preserve cultures of hegemonic masculinity, gatekeep the performance of gender and maintain the sex-based social status of the harasser.[18,19]

There are three broad categories of sex-based harassment: sexual coercion (that is, forced sexual contact), unwanted sexual attention and gender harassment (for example, expressing demeaning attitudes based on a person's gender or sex).[20] Studies have shown that women experience sex-based harassment more often than men do; gender harassment is the most frequent form of sex-based harassment in the workplace; men are more often the perpetrators of sex-based harassment; and incidents are rarely isolated.[21] Lilia Cortina, a professor of psychology with a particular focus on workplace harassment, uses the metaphor of an iceberg to illustrate how sex-based harassment manifests itself at work, with usually only the most egregious forms or the 'tip of the iceberg' being addressed by company policy, and a failure to counteract widespread, lower-level sex-based harassment that lies under the surface and forms the supporting structure for the worst behaviour.[22]

However, sexism in the workplace can't only be accounted for by overtly misogynistic efforts to maintain gender power relations. It also stems from implicit biases and stereotypes that we imbibe through socialisation into our societies and cultures. Violence against women in the form of sexual abuse and harassment is the most extreme form of sexism in the workplace; although it is often poorly monitored, in many jurisdictions there are at least laws in place to prevent and punish this behaviour. More subtle forms of sexist behaviour, on the other hand – from microaggressions through to gendered assumptions about colleagues' priorities, capacity and ability (for example, assuming that a new mother will not want to take on a challenging project) – pervade the workplace and frequently are not recognised as either sexist or as barriers to women's progression.

In a 2022 survey of 5000 women across ten countries, professional services firm Deloitte found that the majority of women

(59 per cent) had experienced harassment or sexist behaviour in the workplace in the past year. The behaviours the women reported included unwanted physical advances, repeated disparaging comments and microaggressions, such as being talked over, interrupted or patronised. Overall, 14 per cent of the women surveyed reported experiencing harassment in the past year, and 50 per cent reported being subject to microaggressions. Not all of these occurrences were brought to the attention of employers; of those respondents who experienced harassment, 66 per cent reported the issue to their employer, and only 23 per cent of experiences of microaggressions were reported. Furthermore, Deloitte found that women in ethnic minority groups and LGBT+ women were more likely to have experienced microaggressions. Another worrying aspect of the survey's findings is that 93 per cent of respondents believed that reporting non-inclusive behaviour would have a negative impact on their careers.[23]

The ubiquity of microaggressions in the workplace is also evidenced by GIWL's 2020 survey conducted with Ipsos, which found that more than one in four men (28 per cent) around the world thought it was acceptable to tell jokes or stories of a sexual nature at work, compared with 16 per cent of women. More than one in eight men (13 per cent) thought it acceptable to display material of a sexual nature at work, almost double the proportion of women (7 per cent) who thought the same.[24]

The extent of sex-based harassment in society, including at work, was brought to global public attention in recent times by the #MeToo social movement. This hashtag was first used by sexual assault survivor and activist Tarana Burke in 2006, but it did not receive widespread attention until late 2017, when actress Alyssa Milano called for women to use social media to share their experiences of sexual abuse. An eruption of women telling their stories and naming perpetrators followed, with the hashtag being used more than 12 million times on Facebook in the 24 hours following Milano's post.[25] The notorious case of Harvey Weinstein and those of other powerful Hollywood men who abused their positions to sexually exploit women made headlines worldwide, but the movement also gave voice to the experiences of women in less high-profile workplaces. Women employed across a variety of sectors including health care, politics, the military and finance joined the collective consciousness-raising, with, for example, women farmworkers expressing solidarity with actresses and drawing attention to an epidemic of misogyny within their own workplaces.[26] The public outpouring by so many women provoked renewed attention on the issue of sex-based harassment in the workplace, and a recognition that employers must do more to protect their staff. Even so, the evidence of endemic sex-based harassment continues to be exposed.

In 2019, the International Bar Association published a report on bullying and sex-based harassment in the legal profession.[27] They surveyed nearly seven thousand members of the profession in 135 countries and the results were shocking: one in three women and one in fourteen men reported having experienced sex-based harassment in a work context. Some 47 per cent of respondents' employers did not have policies in place to address this harassment, and three-quarters of respondents who were victims of sex-based harassment had not reported the incident. The failure to report was attributed to fears of repercussions, the status of the perpetrator and a sense that the behaviour was endemic in the workplace and therefore deemed to be acceptable. Alarmingly, the survey found that harassment was just as likely in workplaces that had relevant policies and training in place as it was in those without, which demonstrates the inadequacy of many 'tick box' approaches to challenging unacceptable behaviour that represent a policy in name only rather than serious consequences for harassers.

The prevalence of sexism and misogyny becomes even more stark when we look at traditionally male-dominated industries such as the primary sector or engineering and construction. A 2017 survey by the Pew Research Center found a slightly higher incidence of sexual harassment of women in male-dominated industries (28 per cent) than female-dominated sectors (20 per cent).[28]

A recent television exposé of the Australian mining industry makes for extremely painful viewing.[29] Interviewees described a horrific culture of sexual coercion that has since led to a parliamentary inquiry in Western Australia. And the problem is not confined to traditionally masculine-heavy industries; these attitudes are also widespread in the tech industry. In 2020, the organisation Women Who Tech conducted a survey of more than one thousand employees, founders and investors in the sector.[30] They found that 48 per cent of women working in tech had experienced harassment, compared to 11 per cent of men. Looking specifically at start-up founders, they found that 44 per cent of women founders said they had experienced harassment, increasing to 47 per cent for women of colour and 65 per cent for LGBT+ founders.

Research and investigations such as these make clear the extent of the problem of sex-based harassment in the workplace, but what are the best measures to tackle it? Addressing sex-based harassment solely through individual grievance procedures – that is, placing the onus on those who have experienced harassment to come forward and report the treatment they have suffered – is problematic: these individualistic solutions tend to leave complainants feeling isolated and vulnerable to repercussions.[31] Because of these concerns, sex-based harassment is widely under-reported, as is frequently demonstrated by responses to anonymous surveys.[32] Furthermore, 'Sexual Harassment 101'–type training that focuses on defining sex-based harassment and outlining how to report it has been shown to be ineffective at leading to changes in behaviour. In contrast, sex-based harassment training that is delivered through human interaction and tailored to the audience for a sustained period of time (four hours or longer) has been shown to be more effective.[33]

The incidence of sex-based harassment in the workplace is sometimes treated as if it is a case of 'a few bad apples'.[34] While it is true that whether an employee is more or less likely to harass their colleagues comes down to the individual, the organisational context is key to limiting their behaviour. The messages sent by senior leaders in terms of modelling inclusive behaviour, rewarding inclusivity and setting out clear consequences for violations have all been shown to make a difference. Calling out or 'calling in' (that is, having a private conversation about) sexist or misogynistic behaviour can also have a positive impact, encouraging self-reflection from the individual on the receiving end of the criticism and increasing the willingness of bystanders to call out such behaviour in the future. Calling out is more effective when it is done calmly and creates a public pressure to avoid non-inclusive behaviour, whereas calling in sends a signal that the intervention is motivated by genuine concern rather than self-aggrandisement on the part of the person instigating the conversation.[35]

Likewise, as sex-based harassment is more common in organisations where men are 'numerically, structurally, or stereotypically dominant',[36] eliminating horizontal and vertical gender segregation by integrating more women throughout an organisation, and promoting diversity more generally, correlates with more inclusive working environments.[37] Sex-based harassment is also more likely to occur in organisations that feature dysfunctional dominance contests, where the culture is of one-upmanship and hyper-competition.[38] These cultures are toxic for everyone within the work environment, not only women.[39] Collaborative, project-based teams rather than hierarchical structures, and promoting empathetic and collective leadership styles, provide a healthier alternative and are associated with positive outcomes for organisations.

On top of sex-based harassment at work, there are numerous structural manifestations of sexism that limit women's career opportunities. My GIWL colleague Rose Cook found that when employers adopt gendered assumptions about their workforce – such as assuming that mothers are not focused on career progression and do not value training opportunities, and that fathers do not have family responsibilities – *all* employees experience lower job quality.[40]

An example of this kind of gendered bias is the expectation that women will become mothers and the assumption that mothers will undertake the majority of unpaid domestic caring work. The result may be that a mother is passed over for career development or promotion, because it is assumed that she will inevitably take maternity leave and may have more demands on her time for caretaking duties than a male colleague, so an employer may unconsciously feel that there is more value in developing her male colleagues.

While these assumptions are certainly not true of all women, and both men and women increasingly have responsibility for caring work, it is still the case that, globally, women undertake three-quarters of unpaid care.[41] As a result, workplaces that valorise overwork by promoting extreme jobs that are not compatible with the other aspects of being human are indirectly sexist and tend to be especially toxic for women, and also damaging for many men.[42] Genuine work flexibility, rather than 'always on' expectations, and understanding and role modelling from senior leadership that colleagues require time to devote to their families, their personal lives and their physical and mental health (and, of course, sufficient sleep) are essential to fostering and sustaining inclusive working cultures.

Another form of subtle sexism that can manifest in the workplace is gender stereotyping about what 'good' looks like. One area where women are disadvantaged in this manner relates to the competence/confidence debate. In his persuasive and provocative book *Why Do So Many Incompetent Men Become Leaders? (And how to fix it)*, Tomas Chamorro-Premuzic suggests that overconfidence is too often mistaken for competence and this puts women at a disadvantage. He argues that men are more often socialised to be narcissistic leaders and that the self-belief this generates is attractive, as it fits with commonly held stereotypes of a good leader: the strong man at the top of a hierarchy. In fact, research suggests that the most effective leaders are humble and empathetic, and that collective leadership is more productive in the workplace than individualistic, authoritarian styles. These biases make it more likely that self-asserting men will be selected as leaders, even when they perform poorly on measures of competence when compared with many women, or with more self-reflective or introverted men.[43]

The use of gendered language is another way that biases can influence women's career progression. For example, studies have found that when job advertisements use stereotypically 'masculine' words such as 'driven' or 'competitive', women are less attracted to these jobs than they are to exactly the same job described using stereotypically 'feminine' words such as 'collaborative' or 'committed'. In one study, men and women both assumed that a workplace would be more male-dominated when the job advertisement included masculine words.[44] My GIWL colleague Laura Jones worked with LinkedIn to analyse how men and women respond to and use language in the world of work, including during job searches, in interviews and when talking about their roles. LinkedIn found that 44 per cent of women would be discouraged from applying for a role if the word 'aggressive' was in the job description, but only a third of men felt the same.[45] Clearly, this evidence suggests that checking the language of job advertisements to ensure that it is attractive to a diverse pool of candidates is a necessary step to create more inclusive recruitment processes.

Beyond the recruitment stage, lack of a sense of fit or belonging can have a gendered aspect and can influence higher rates of exit or lower rates of ambition among women employees. Studies of UK police services found that women and men reported similar levels of ambition when they entered the service, but that a gender gap emerged over time.[46] Another study found that women police officers perceived a mismatch between their own character traits (for example, being collaborative and sociable) and those they attributed to senior officers (decisive, assertive, arrogant), and that this sense of lack of fit was a significant predictor of a reduced level of ambition and a higher propensity to exit the workforce.[47] These findings reinforce the importance of fostering inclusive cultures within organisations that move beyond masculine stereotypes of the good leader, and model a diversity of leadership styles.

Another area where bias contributes to unequal outcomes for men and women is in the association between performance and reward. A 2015 meta-analysis of 142 studies looking at performance evaluations and rewards in a variety of work settings found no average differences between men's and women's performance evaluations, but large differences in men's advantage in terms of salaries, bonuses and promotions. The performance–reward gap was larger in highly prestigious and male-dominated occupations; in industries with higher proportions of female executives, salaries were more commensurate with performance.[48]

Gender stereotypes have also been shown to limit women's opportunities at work when it comes to salary negotiations. There is a received wisdom that women don't ask for pay rises or negotiate higher salaries at the recruitment stage because they lack confidence, but more recent evidence suggests that women's reluctance stems from their awareness that they will be judged more harshly than men for seeking a higher salary. In one study, researchers conducted a randomised control trial with candidates by altering whether advertisements stated that wages were negotiable. They found that when there was no explicit statement, men were more likely to negotiate for higher wages than women, but when the job description explicitly stated that wages were negotiable there was no gender gap in the likelihood to negotiate.[49]

In a 2019 review of the evidence about barriers to women's career progression, Laura Jones of GIWL concluded that, 'In the absence of clear systems and transparent systems, decisions about pay and promotion are more likely to be made through processes that disadvantage women, including via [male-dominated] networks and the process of social cloning, where those in positions of power champion those who are like themselves.'[50]

Research suggests that trying to eliminate implicit biases through training that raises awareness of bias is often ineffective at leading to behaviour change and can even backfire.[51,52] However, we can attempt to de-bias processes to reduce the impact of biases on our decisions. A classic example that is often cited to illustrate the potential power of de-biasing processes is the case of orchestra auditions.[53] In the 1970s and 1980s, orchestras began to conduct 'blind' auditions, in which a screen was introduced in front of the performers so that they were not visible to the selectors. Researchers undertook a study to assess the difference the screen made. The number of participants in the study was small, which limited the researchers' ability to draw strong conclusions, but, following the widespread adoption of such auditions, they found an improvement in women's success in auditions, and women's representation in orchestras increased.[54,55]

In most workplaces, placing a screen before potential hires is not a realistic solution – but there are numerous alternatives that can help to eliminate the distorting impact of bias, such as using anonymised CVs in the early stage of sifting through applicants, gathering multiple independent reviews with candidate ratings, and designing the interview process with the intention to measure job-related competencies rather than relying only on face-to-face panel interviews, where gender stereotypes more often influence our decision-making.

It is sometimes suggested that efforts to raise women's confidence – or, to look at it another way, to 'fix women', as if they are the problem – are the key to counteracting misogyny and sexism, including subtle sexism, experienced by women in the workplace. Although these efforts might go some way to improving women's sense of self-efficacy, the examples we have seen in this chapter show that these efforts alone will not create more fair and inclusive workplaces. We must also counteract the structural and individual biases that hold women back. In addition, providing leadership training programs for women that are distinct tracks, apart from more integrated networking opportunities, may provide safe spaces for women to share their experiences and build networks for collective action, but they are unlikely to reduce the systemic barriers that stand in the way of women's career progression.

•

So, if we have now seen the scale of the problem, and some of the massive body of evidence documenting sexism and misogyny in the workplace, what are the solutions we can look to in order to make progress?

The Global Institute for Women's Leadership has produced a report about what really works when it comes to ensuring an inclusive working environment for all staff employed in formal workplaces. The report was based on a review of the evidence from more than sixty pieces of academic literature, drawn mainly from 'in-workplace', or real-world, research. Our key recommendations for employers were:

- Focus on both prevention and promotion when it comes to fostering an inclusive working environment, which means emphasising diversity and inclusion as important company values as well as providing robust systems for addressing poor behaviour.
- Deploy diversity and inclusion training that focuses on behaviour change, active learning and promoting dialogue between

colleagues who wouldn't usually connect. This training should include proactive participation from trainees, and support them to break habits that show unconscious bias.

- Encourage employee networks and diversity taskforces, which can increase the success of other diversity initiatives by providing a support network, championing the cause and holding leadership to account.

- Emphasise to employees that confronting non-inclusive behaviour is a 'community responsibility' that should be shared by all, and support staff to be 'active bystanders' who feel obligated and supported to calmly call out bad behaviour.

- Support leaders and managers to model inclusive behaviour in their conduct, values and interactions.

- Ensure all corporate communications celebrate diversity. Taking an 'identity conscious' approach to how an organisation is discussed and portrayed is proven to be more effective than an 'identity blind' model, which does not highlight and embrace difference.

- Ensure that wider systems around recruitment, retention and progression are unbiased and fair.[56]

If all workplaces were to adopt these practices, it would be a big step forward in making the world of formal work more inclusive for women and for all.

As we acknowledged earlier, formal workplaces do not give the full picture of women's work globally, and women working in the informal economy largely do not have recourse to any of these change-making practices. In order to protect all women from sex-based harassment at work, and to create improved working cultures for all, governments need to take steps to help workers transition to the formal economy and to protect those who work outside of it. Governments and NGOs should also facilitate women working in the informal economy to organise, and support existing women's collectives.[57] Other steps that national governments should take in order to improve conditions for informal and under-protected workers are to make progress on the International Labour Organization's Domestic Workers Convention, 2011; to ensure that domestic work in private households is fully recognised as real work; and to fully implement international standards that recognise the human rights of agricultural wage workers.[58]

Misogyny and sexism continue to shape women's experiences of paid and unpaid work, and to hinder advances towards gender equality. However, these behaviours have not gone unchallenged: women, and men, are increasingly calling out bad behaviour and organising to demand change. While feminist campaigns such as the #MeToo movement have brought home the alarming scale of sex-based harassment in the workplace, they have also demonstrated the potential of collective action to bring misogyny to public attention and to generate momentum for solution-focused advocacy.

Governments have responded by introducing and reinforcing gender equality legislation, adopting international targets, measuring progress and setting expectations for employers (see, for example, my colleague Minna Cowper-Coles' report comparing gender pay gap reporting regimes).[59] Supranational organisations such as the ILO and the UN are driving the international agenda by conducting research, setting global goals and galvanising international support. NGOs, trade unions and academic researchers continue to collect evidence and campaign for action. Employers of goodwill are designing and implementing policies to tackle sex-based harassment and de-bias processes.

There is a significant risk of failure to make progress, or even of backsliding, if global challenges such as climate change, the rise of populist politics and the impact of the war in Ukraine shift public attention away from women's rights. However, resurgent feminist organising has the power to remind us all that these problems will not be addressed without the full involvement of women. In order to ensure that women's experience and perspectives are incorporated into attempts to limit climate change and to generate sustainable economies, we need to bring our knowledge of what works to create inclusive environments into our workplaces, campaigns and daily lives.

Female leaders are judged by a different standard. Show emotion and we are 'weak'; hold ourselves in check and we are 'cold'. Julia and I are from different ends of the political spectrum. We led countries on opposite sides of the world. Yet our experiences are the same. With her speech, Julia exposed that double standard with a clarity and an honesty that reached far beyond the House of Representatives and the domestic politics of the time. Ten years on, we still have some way to go, but after Julia's speech we could no longer say we didn't know.

Theresa May, UK Member of Parliament for Maidenhead
and former Prime Minister of the United Kingdom

'What's the worst misogyny you've had to deal with in your career?' Responses from *A Podcast of One's Own*

I feel as if I have faced a lot of misogyny, particularly being a girl Wiggle. But I don't really worry about it, or I'm not affected by it. I know that social media can be such a negative place, but it can also be such a positive place to connect with families as well.

Emma Watkins, formerly known as 'Emma Wiggle'/Yellow Wiggle

Part Three

FIGHTING MISOGYNY

Chapter 10

What do next-generation activists think? In conversation with Chanel Contos, Caitlin Figueiredo and Sally Scales

Julia Gillard

As all of the chapters in this book make painfully clear, misogyny remains pervasive and deep-seated. It is not just going to disappear like morning dew because we are shining a light on it. Changing the stereotypes and structures in our society that hold women back is hard work, and it takes time. Despite the efforts made by so many to accelerate this progress, at the current rate of change, the World Economic Forum estimates it will take 136 years for us to reach gender equality globally.[1]

Against that kind of depressing backdrop, it would be easy for younger women to say, 'Why even bother?'; for them to look at older feminists such as me and say, 'You have laboured and failed to create a fair world, free from misogyny – why should we waste our lives trying?' Instead, they could choose to navigate the world as best they can, trying to avoid the worst traps and pitfalls created by gender inequality without campaigning for major change.

When I first left political office, I would frequently hear an eerie echo of this kind of thinking. Young women would approach me and say that watching my time in politics and all the sexist slurs and misogynist hate I'd endured had put them off becoming involved. It was hugely saddening for me to confront the very real risk that my role modelling had amounted not to a call to arms, but rather to sounding out the call to retreat.

And yet, in more recent years, I have detected a change. The news seems to be flooded with younger women who are living their feminism visibly and vibrantly, leading campaigns for change with a savvy, take-no-shit attitude. This is the kind of feminism Abbey Hansen captured so brilliantly in her TikTok video, mouthing the words of the misogyny speech as she applies her make-up and steels herself to go out into the world with the lyrics 'I'm a bitch, I'm a boss' pounding in the background.

I now have hope that another feminist wave is gathering, drawing on the power of new activists, who are unapologetic about the need for change. But how real is all this? What is today's feminism? Who is fighting misogyny now?

To answer these questions, I spoke to three young Australian activists: Chanel Contos, Caitlin Figueiredo and Sally Scales. Let me introduce them to you.

Chanel holds a first-class master's degree in gender, education and international development from University College London. For her dissertation, she investigated sexual assaults on girls who were high school students, focusing on abuse where the perpetrator was also school-aged. When she reached out to students from a limited number of elite girls' schools in Australia to ask for survivors' stories, she was blown away by the mountain of responses she received. Ultimately, more than six thousand survivor testimonies were submitted. This led Chanel to become the founder and CEO of Teach Us Consent, which gathered 44,000 signatures on an online petition demanding effective consent education reform in Australian schools. This activism has triggered change to policy regulating schools and teaching practices.

Caitlin is the founder and CEO of Jasiri Australia, a youth-led social enterprise on a mission to unleash a fearless generation of women and girls. At 22, Caitlin was listed on the *Forbes* '30 Under 30 Asia' list for co-founding the Girls Takeover Parliament program, a bipartisan initiative that promotes representational democracy and increasing female political participation across the Asia-Pacific region. Her advocacy efforts in youth development and gender equality have been recognised nationally and internationally, with Caitlin being invited to the first *Forbes* Under 30 Global Women's Summit. Caitlin is also the co-chair of the Australian Youth Affairs Coalition and has sat on three United Nations task forces.

Sally is a Pitjantjatjara woman from Pipalyatjara, in the far west of the Anangu Pitjantjatjara Yankunytjatjara (APY) Lands in remote South Australia. She was elected as chairperson of the APY Executive Board Council in 2019, the second woman to have held this position. An artist herself and winner of the 2022 Roberts Family Prize, Sally has worked with the APY Art Centre Collective since 2013 in cultural liaison, elder support and spokesperson roles. Sally is part of the leadership team advocating for the Uluru Statement from the Heart, which captures the largest consensus of First Nations peoples on a proposal for reform and recognition in Australian history.[2] On top of all of these commitments, Sally is a foster mum to Walter, who is now six years old.

We begin our discussions with where they were and how they felt when they first heard the misogyny speech. Caitlin says:

'I first heard the misogyny speech when I was fifteen and in high school. At the time I was sort of interested in politics but wasn't active. My friends said, "Caitlin, did you hear this?", so we got around the computer – all my friends, about ten of us – and we started watching it.

I remember my mouth dropped! I was looking at you and I was feeling everything that you were feeling – the anger, the passion, the hatred, the frustration, and I felt like, "Oh my god! Finally, someone is saying something." All my friends and I were so shocked and saying, "Yeah, we feel seen."

I didn't know about "misogyny" until your speech. I had to go and look it up, but I already felt that women and girls were treated differently. I remember quite clearly that at the start of primary school, our teacher asked, "What do you want to be when you grow up?" I raised my hand and said, "I will be the Prime Minister of Australia one day," and all the boys laughed. They were like, "Ha ha, Caitlin, there's never been a female prime minister." And I was like, "Can't I be the first?" They all said, "No, that doesn't happen."

When you became prime minister, that attitude instantly shifted. But then I could see that the level of respect, the comments, and even the questions that you were given, weren't the same as for previous male prime ministers.

Watching the speech, I was thinking, "Okay, you know what? There are people who get it. There are people who are willing to actually call out bad behaviour." That was a massive turning point for me and my friends.'

Sally was with friends in Alice Springs when she first saw the misogyny speech. She came to that moment steeped in women's leadership. She says:

'*In my formative years, my mother was the chair of Ngaanyatjarra Pitjantjatjara Yankunytjatjara Women's Council, which is based in Central Australia. The women weren't part of the conversation in the 1980s around getting land rights. These are strong, staunch, Black women, but the government effectively said to them, "We're just going to talk to the men about what we're doing." In reply, the women said, "Well, we'll start our own organisation." I grew up seeing that incredible leadership and seeing how that duality happened: the iron fist with a bit of a smile. My mum's got the biggest sass, I get it from her. I've seen how she uses it.*

I remember watching the lead-up to the misogyny speech, and that time was filled with rage. You were our leader, but you were getting such hate and disgusting commentary, which just didn't seem to end, ever. It also showed me that there was a lack of leadership by everyone else because they allowed that commentary to go on and go on and go on.

So, the misogyny speech was just like a "Hell yeah!" moment. It had that power for me, the reaffirming that we can just be anything, and, you know what? Everyone else might not lean in. Everyone else might not stand up, but we do. Women constantly stand up. Women constantly are the drivers for change. Women constantly are the ones who say, "Enough is enough, this is not going to be the way we do it."

It's the way you managed to do that – it could have been done in such a way that everyone would have been like, "Oh, she's a hysterical woman." But it was just done in a way that was so powerful and brilliant. And it's like you saying to the sexists, "I know you are going to keep going. I can see it on your faces. But I'm not moving. You can't move me, and this is what my leadership is." I just felt that was the most powerful thing.

I think all Australian women walked a little bit taller that day. It was a bit like, "Our prime minister has gone there. Do you wanna go there? We know how to go there now.'"

Chanel remembers the misogyny speech as leading to far deeper conversations about gender equality in her life. She says:

'I think I was in my living room and I heard the speech on the news. I had just come home from school and I was fourteen years old. This was a time in my life where the dictating, coercive forces of gender inequality that victimise girls and women were at the peak for me in terms of how I saw myself and how I interacted with my peers and boys and the world around me. It was kind of a time where I was meant to feel, "Oh yeah, women are subordinate to men," because that's what I was being told by everything around me. I grew up in quite a right-wing, conservative household.

I had become numb to all the negative media around you as prime minister. This was the first moment when I realised, "Oh, that's not okay and that's not what should be happening." Because I grew up with you being prime minister, I did think women could be prime minister, but I had never thought about whether women could be prime minister without facing all this backlash.

I didn't know what "misogyny" was, actually, until your speech. I had never heard that word before, I don't think, which is so disappointing, given that I went to an all-girls school, where I would have hoped we might have had these conversations earlier.

The next day at school I remember a friend talking to me about the speech, and also the head girl of the school. Then all our friends were talking about it, and we were getting that sense of community that is so important to women. We created a conversation in a safe space.'

I am a big believer that while it can be intriguing to talk about the past, what really matters is what we learn from it and how it leads to change in the future. As a result, I am keen to dig a little deeper and find out how these incredible young women see their feminism. In answer to that question, Chanel says:

'Feminism is equality, which sounds like a boring answer. But I also see feminism as being very deconstructive and critical of the current status quo, because, in order to achieve true feminism, which would be equality, we need radical change. I pursue that very specifically with initiatives such as the Teach Us Consent campaign, trying to prevent men's violence against women and children, but also more broadly, creating conversations and trying to change cultures and things like that, because I feel as if it's all the micro stuff which builds up that's kind of getting in the way of real change. So, again in my conservative Greek family household, it's things being said like, "Oh, that's a good job for a woman," or "Oh, that's a bad job for a woman."

My focus in promoting feminism is very much on education. I have studied feminism now at high academic levels, but my original teachers in feminism were other girls at school. I'd never read a feminist text in my life or any sort of feminist book at that age. It was very much what I learnt in my immediate group of friends. I would say probably there were two or three who seemed to be equipped with this stuff from earlier on in their lives, presumably from their family environment. They were the ones who told our whole friendship group we shouldn't be using the word "slut". They were the ones who, when boys from neighbouring schools said horrible things, stood up and were willing to "boycott" them or encourage us to say something about it.

I do remember one teacher making our whole history class get up and stand next to the window and look over at the boys' schools while she said, "They're going to earn more than you." She talked us through the gender pay gap and why it happens. But my early feminism was mainly learnt from my peers, and I was most receptive to it when it came from my peers. I also like to think that, over time, I was involved in spreading and teaching feminism, and that is what matters to me so much now.'

Caitlin endorses the concept that feminism is equality, but goes on to say:

'I think feminism for me is about reclaiming and healing the past, peeling away trauma that has been passed down through genera-tions. I'm Anglo-Indian and I grew up in a very patriarchal society where, from the time that I was little, whenever all my aunties and uncles would get together, all the boys were put on pedestals. I remember our aunties would sit around, literally in a circle, and the boys were always brought into the middle of the circle, and my aunties would go, "Look at how well my son is doing. He has won all of these awards. He's fantastic. Oh, this is what he's going to do when he is grown up," and the girls would always just sit there around the outside of the circle. That never really changed and so I always felt very, very small.

I am also a survivor of quite horrific domestic violence. I kept that to myself for almost two decades. The first time ever I spoke about it, I remember being on stage at the 100 Women of Influence awards, and I looked down and my hero, Natasha Stott Despoja, was sitting at one of the first tables in the crowd. I've loved her since I was a little girl. I was like, You know what? This is my moment where I'm going to speak about why I'm doing this. I'm here because I have been silenced my whole life and I know what it's like to feel powerless – to have your identity, to have your sense of security taken from you. To be on the verge between life or death because someone feels that they have the right to take that from you. That's why I'm here in this moment, because I don't want any other young woman, any other girl, no matter where they are in Australia or abroad, to go through this.

For me, that's sort of why I do it, and that's why I am really passionate about politics and making sure that we have diversity of faces and lived experiences there – because, yes, individual conversations are so, so important. Education is so damn important. But legislation, policy, changing the structures of our society can make a life-or-death difference. That's what I'm trying to do through Girls Takeover Parliament, through the Australian Youth Affairs Coalition – bringing real people with real experiences together with legislative people.

Except for public speeches, I've never really spoken to my family about what happened to me as a child, especially, my broader family. I was just in Singapore, two nights ago, on my way back from overseas and I sat down to speak with one of my uncles over a bottle of wine. We started talking about our family history. I was like, "Do you know what happened to me when I was a child?" He said, "No, what happened to you?" I said, "Well, when I was a girl, my life was almost taken by a family member because I was born a girl, because I was not dressing the way they thought I should, because I was speaking out, and this was happening in the suburbs of Perth." He looked at me and said, "Oh my god! I can't believe that this has happened to you," but then he told me stories he had heard about his mother and her mother, and it's that generational trauma that has been passed down consistently that we need to overcome.

We have a long way to go, but that's what it's about for me. It's about reclaiming those stories, about exposing them, and about trying to fix them and heal them.'

The power of these words hits me – how could they not? But I am also curious about Caitlin's connection to former Australian politician Natasha Stott Despoja, given that, doing the maths, Caitlin would have just been born when Natasha was prominent in politics. In a heartwarming aside, Caitlin explains she met Natasha at the time when she was the Australian Ambassador for Women and Girls, a special international advocacy role promoting gender equality and women's empowerment, and the human rights of women and girls. Caitlin describes:

'I was doing a lot of work around the UN, so I'd hear her speak there. Then I started tagging her on Twitter – "I'm doing this" and "I'm doing that. I really want to meet you." The first time I met her, I was in Parliament House and I saw that Natasha was coming through the security area. I was with my friend Hannah and we were like, "Hi Natasha, it's so nice to meet you," and she said, "Are you Caitlin from Twitter?" She has been my mentor ever since. She's the most phenomenal, incredible woman I've ever met. I don't know how she keeps doing what she does. She just inspires me every day.'

After we all share a laugh about 'Caitlin from Twitter', I then turn to Sally to hear about her understanding of feminism. She explains:

'I mean, it is that element of equality and what that looks like. But for me, my own feminism has been about becoming more and more aware of how, in the Western world, the valuation of men is held above that of women. I hate the word "Dreamtime", so I always talk about our culture, in which there's always been a recognition of the importance of both women and men; their laws and cultures are seen as being on equal footing. The men's stuff needs the support of the women.

I also grew up with my Dad when we were in Alice Springs, because Mum wanted to live at home, in her country. I have two strong parents who really pushed for me to have that duality in our language, duality in our cultures.

The biggest moment for me was when I was twelve and I was told by a family member that, as a First Nations person, I already have one foot in the grave. That was a huge shock to me, but it was a serious message about our life expectancy, the chronic ill health experienced by First Nations people and all the systems that are built up to fail us. I had to think, Oh wow, okay. So how do I then manage that and steel myself? How do I lean in? How do I be that advocate, be that voice?

As I said, I'm really privileged: I had all my language and my culture very firmly attached to my being. I had incredible leaders and elders, male and female, but especially the male leaders who quickly elevated me into leadership roles on bodies like the APY Executive Council.

I am grateful for that, but I became more and more aware of the lack of equality in work spaces, constantly walking into the room and seeing you are the only woman, or you are the only person of colour. I always talk about how one is a token, two is a change.

Women have always been leaders. I think that's what my feminism is about. It's about saying, "No, no, no, I actually belong in this space. You're just catching up to me," and then turning that spotlight onto the other women who don't have that or need that support.

My biggest thing is actually seeing who's not in the room and who do we need to make sure is in the room. It's about, how do I use my privilege and power for the other ones that need it? I am always thinking through questions about how to be a good ally. I talk to others about it and urge them to stand there, next to that person, and say, "Hang on, do you need my help? Do you need my support?"

And then you can deal with marginalising behaviours. You can pull a person up and say, "Hey, I just heard your comment over there, that's really incredibly rude and we can't have that in this space anymore." It's about what standard you are going to be okay with.'

There is a core of agreement here between each of these younger activists – that feminism is about true equality – but such a diversity of context and views about what gets prioritised. Being prepared to educate and having the courage to challenge are common themes. I ask myself whether that is different from the feminism of the past and find myself thinking no, it is not. However, today's reality is different to any other time in history, with much more understanding of the way gender, race and other forms of discrimination intersect.

That is progress; and yet, when we look at gender equality generally, the degree and pace of change has been maddeningly slow. I want to understand how frustrating being a feminist is today for the coming generation, given we ought to be bequeathing to them a far more equal world than we are actually passing on.

Caitlin admits she has had moments of doubt, and is particularly troubled by assaults on the ability of women to make their own reproductive choices, saying:

'Literally I feel so gross when I look at what's happening in the United States, with the challenges to access to abortion. Men, and even some very conservative women, are almost like, "We have a key to your body, we have the key to your future and only we can unlock it." That for me is really, really difficult. I remember saying to friends, "I am losing a little bit of hope now that I'm getting older," because of setbacks in Australia and around the world.

But mostly I am more optimistic than that. I do honestly think that in twenty to thirty years' time, when our generation and the next generations coming through are in the majority, there will be major change. There is a movement building which is moving away from capitalism, from being all about money and greed. Now people are asking, "All right, how can we take care of each other? How can we start tackling climate change? How can we stop thinking about us in the here and now and start thinking about the next seven generations, ten generations? Younger people are starting to think that way. They're not taking the jobs that can get them the fanciest car but the ones that make the biggest amount of difference. It's not going to be immediate, but profound change is coming.'

Chanel describes herself as being positive, and for a similar reason. She believes Australia, specifically, is at a pivotal moment of accelerated change, saying:

'The reason I'm optimistic is because the younger generations are better than the older generations at unlearning, reflecting and understanding. Once Australians learn how to unlearn, and once it becomes normal to self-reflect in that way and critique cultures and current practices, I think it's going to be a really fast transition towards something a lot better. I hope that does have an intersectional approach.

I do have concerns – and I know I've also been a part of this – that mainstream feminism in Australia, or the feminism that the media gives attention to, is predominantly white feminism. While I'm optimistic for the future, we are at risk of not changing the structures as a whole and not actually deconstructing these power imbalances across all sections of society. We're at risk of going towards a very neoliberal feminism that is inherently capitalistic in that way.

I talk about rape culture a lot in my movement and I say we have all been complacent. When you are being complacent, you're being complicit, and we need to actively do better.

That's the kind of approach that drives anti-racism work. With all of the work and conversations that the Black Lives Matter movement generated, for example, it started to become normal to accept that to be anti-racist you must understand that you are living and working within a society that is racist. When I speak to my parents, they would say, "I'm not racist." But it's not helpful to this conversation to just pretend that you don't see race.

If we continue to develop the understanding that just because you as an individual are not doing something, it doesn't mean that you don't benefit from the system built around it, people will increasingly have a higher social conscience. That means I do hope for better, but I also understand my limited echo chamber, so that optimism might be misplaced.'

Sally is also optimistic, but she too worries about complacency. She recounts receiving a powerful new insight in recent weeks. A colleague built on the expression 'We have to break the glass ceiling,' by adding 'but we also have to elevate the floor.' That has stayed with Sally, who explains:

'If you're in a minority, and you end up being the spokesperson, you know – "This is the Aboriginal leader . . ." blah blah blah blah, then no one ever has any critical thought about that person or those systems. They just sit in that place of complacency.

Yes, we need some more female representatives. Yes, we need some more people of colour representatives. But I would always say whoever we put up as those faces of leadership, we all have to have some critical thinking about them because it's not good enough to just have someone there.

Instead, we need to make sure we do our research, because it's one thing to break that glass ceiling, but we have to start raising the floor and elevating all of us. It's about bringing everyone together now.

It's not about waiting for someone to step into that space of leadership when they're hitting a certain age. It is time now for everyone to move in, and we go together. Women have always gone together. Women have said, "I've got you. I see you. Let's go."

You know that even when you are young. For example, when you're a teenager, when you go out with your friends and you see a girl and you don't feel comfortable leaving her because she is a little bit too drunk, you say to her, "We have you and let's get you home safe."

Sally's anecdote reminds Chanel of a personal experience, and she says:

'*Two nights ago, I was walking down my street quite late at night. There was someone walking a few metres in front of me. I couldn't tell if it was a man or a woman and I was wary. Then she turned around and saw me. I could tell that she was also worried that I was walking behind her until we saw each other. I said, "I swear I am not following you," and she said "No, I know. I'm so glad that you're also a girl." We both just laughed because this was a moment of relief, like, "Ah! you're not a man."*'

Sally replies, '*It's sad that we think that. It's sad the way we go there. But it's also a protective mechanism.*'

This remarkable younger generation is communal and caring, full of understanding about the risk of gendered violence. While this still-harsh world for women could easily wear away their optimism, it has not. They have a degree of confidence that change is coming in the next few decades.

To round off our discussion, I ask for comments on two aspects of the emerging feminism that have struck me. First, it is clear from what has been said so far that these younger feminists tend to view the gender equality project as one which is not about individual women changing themselves, but about changing the current power structures. I want to know whether in their minds it is about reaching equality in terms of who gets to the top of the pyramid, or is the aim to reshape hierarchies altogether?

Then, with the words to the old feminist song in my mind – 'Don't be too polite, girls, don't be too polite!' – I reflect on whether, despite this injunction, those of us who have gone before may have been too polite. I ask, is this current generation far more likely to make demands with real forcefulness, and make it clear that they are not prepared to take it anymore?

I think of these as unrelated but interesting questions; however, Chanel weaves them together, saying:

'My mum grew up in a really conservative, strict Greek house-hold, and she chose to marry my dad because the other guy that she wanted to marry wouldn't let her go to university. I remember when I was young thinking, "Oh, she's become a really successful lawyer, and that's amazing. That's, like, women's empowerment." But it's not really, because that only changed things for her, not the broader picture.

I feel as if it's very rare for a young woman to have an idea of just their own personal success without thinking about woman-hood as a whole. I also think that ties in to why we could be less polite, and why we don't need to be polite, because there's this whole generation of people backing us, even if our parents don't agree with the way that we're speaking about things or asking for things, and the language we're using on TV, we know that there are people our age who relate to us, who want to make change. I think it's easier to go against those institutional values of what a nice, polite, ladylike girl should be when we know that we have the backing of true sisterhood.'

Caitlin adds:

'*Actually, one of your comments, Julia, reminds me of a time when a very senior government minister invited me to a round-table discussion because I have expertise in the Pacific and supporting young people to be entrepreneurs.*

I was answering all these questions, but three times in a row the minister stopped me and repeated everything that I had just said, in his own words. The fourth time it happened, I interrupted him with the words, "Excuse me, please do not cut me off. They all know what I'm saying." I was never invited back to that minister's office again.

That behaviour towards women, which happened constantly, had just been accepted because he was a minister. He was someone in a very senior position of power. But for me, that was a real catalyst moment with me deciding, I'm not going to let you devalue what I'm trying to say or why I'm here.

For me, this next phase of feminism is about standing up for ourselves, and not just changing the structures but dismantling them and rebuilding them. I feel this next wave of feminism is going to be all about making sure that every voice is at the table, and if it's not, we are going to extend the table as far as possible. If we have to smash walls down to open the space, we will do that.'

Chanel builds on Caitlin's words, saying:

'*What we are dealing with at the moment is old power, which is held by a few heavily controlled and inaccessible elites. Essentially the traditional parliament system is old power. Whereas this younger generation, we've harnessed technologies like social media, and that means we can communicate en masse, we can shift discourse overnight. One video can go viral and we can suddenly have a unified understanding of a new moral good across our whole generation instantly. I think this kind of new power is continuously being harnessed and it is inclusive, it's accessible. It's not elite.'*

Sally takes a different tack:

'I think there's an incredible myth out there that all women have to agree, that all First Nations people have to agree, that all minorities have to agree. When people make that mistake, I always turn around and say, "Well, do all white people love Pauline Hanson and agree with what she has to say?", and that shocks them because she is a very divisive politician in Australia.

We live in a democracy, but we need to be critical, we need to be thinking, what is the end goal here? My thing is, what is your core goal? Keeping that really front and centre matters, because everyone loves adding in other ideas and then we get really busy and we don't know what's going on anymore. You sort of have to rein it back and go, okay, what is our core business?

I'm really bossy and pushy. What I love about the younger generation is they are saying, "We have seen the skill sets of the older ones and seen what they've tried to do, and we're really going to push through.' I think that's what is really amazing.

Where your speech was really powerful, Julia, was that it was effectively saying, "I'm letting you know that I'm throwing down the rules, I'm putting a boundary on this." It also pushed everyone else to go, "Actually, I'm deeply disappointed in myself that I didn't move in, and I didn't lean in, and I didn't say this was a problem." I think it means that everyone is now saying, "Actually, standing back is not good enough for me anymore."'

I end the conversation having learnt a great deal and feeling truly emotional, knowing that the future is in safe hands – and also knowing I will never hear a higher accolade for the misogyny speech than Sally's closing words. I cannot entirely agree with her that now everyone is no longer standing back, but I love the youthful enthusiasm behind her words. If she is right that it has generated that reaction in some, and that there is more activism than there would have been as a result, that is more than enough for me.

I was in my first year of university when I heard Prime Minister Julia Gillard's famed misogyny speech. It cut through the standard rhetoric of politics and seemed to speak directly to the lived experiences of Australian women. Most Question Time performances went largely ignored by the public, but this was very different.

It had been a year marred by sexist headlines, inappropriate comments by MPs and off-colour jokes by the media – often at the prime minister's expense and always in reference to gender. The prime minister's words resonated with me and with so many other people who, through the political discourse, felt disrespected and maligned on the basis of their sex. It was a rallying cry to women across the country, that sexism should be called out and that we 'are entitled to a better standard than this'.

Brittany Higgins, former political staffer and
Visiting Fellow at the Global Institute for Women's Leadership

Being in the House of Representatives chamber as Julia Gillard made her misogyny speech felt like a moment separate from time. I knew I'd witnessed an earthquake, and I knew there would be after-shocks. The sentiments Julia expressed came from deep under the surface, but they weren't only Julia's frustrations. Like the Marches for Justice that took place in 2021, they were the frustrations of every woman who had done what women who are being attacked or overlooked at work are told to do: stay calm, follow the rules, be polite and affable, smile, do your job better than the boys, and eventually people will recognise and reward your professionalism. Julia had set that tone for the government, too: we wouldn't 'play the gender card' by calling out Tony Abbott's relentless sexism and bullying – we would just govern, and do it calmly and competently. And there was Tony Abbott, after all the pornographic slurs he had allowed on our prime minister, actually accusing her of sexism. Well. Enough is enough.

Watching Julia that day was like watching a Valkyrie rise above the clouds, or Boudicca ride across the plain in her chariot. But it was deeply meaningful because she wasn't speaking for herself. She was speaking for every woman who has been good at her job but under-mined by sexism. She was speaking for every woman who has been told to ignore the taunts and just get on with it. She was speaking for every woman, because she was speaking about every woman's experience. That's why two million people watched the speech in the first two weeks after it was delivered. That's why young women on TikTok can recite the speech. It's why it's on tea towels. Julia's frustration, like that of the women who marched in March 2021, is an articulate, compelling expression of what every woman feels for her daughter, her sister, her mother, her colleague, her friend and for herself: enough. Enough.

Tanya Plibersek, Australian Member of
Parliament for Sydney

Chapter 11

Misogyny:
What's next?

Julia Gillard

As these essays have revealed, misogyny is both as old as time and as modern as a tweet.

It continues to pervade workplaces, influence media reporting and shape politics. Misogyny still appears in its traditional forms, as well as shapeshifting as technology and social norms change.

Misogyny allies itself with racism and other forms of discrimination, so that women who are already facing prejudice and exclusion endure more of it.

Misogyny is the fist that strikes a woman's body and the belief that women's bodies are not their own. That women's consent doesn't matter. That women should not have the right to make their own reproductive choices.

For women, living with misogyny is like walking through the world being forced to carry an unwanted burden. We are so used to this baggage, most of the time we don't even recognise how heavy it is.

Women everywhere are weighed down by misogyny, but the degree of gender inequality women confront varies from nation to nation, community to community. For billions of women, poverty and the denial of basic rights, such as getting to go to school, cement gender inequality and rob them of choices and opportunities. A vital part of our feminist mission is showing solidarity with and giving support to these women, many of whom are courageously campaigning for change.

Billions of other women today have more options available to them than their mothers or grandmothers could have imagined in their wildest dreams, yet they do not live in a gender equal world. Instead, when looking up, they see a glass ceiling, and at the same time the floor they stand on feels wobbly because hard-won advances, including reproductive rights, can be taken away.

And women still have to instinctively make the day-to-day adjustments misogyny requires. How many times have you or someone you know calibrated behaviour because of it? Like leaving a party early, because bad things happen to women late at night. Or staying silent, because speaking up means being characterised as a nasty bitch. Or holding yourself back from taking on visible roles because of the abuse you've witnessed directed at women in public life.

Mostly these decisions are made without clear and conscious thought. Instead, in microseconds, we do what women have always had to do. We shape ourselves in response to the cues we have been given our whole lives about who we should be.

Women don't do this because we lack confidence or need training. Women don't need *fixing*. Instead, we do it because the world is infused with misogyny. It is there in society's structures, which have been overwhelmingly made by men, for men, and in our cultural stereotypes, which dictate narrow and restrictive modes of womanhood, and invite repercussions on women who dare to step out of the mould.

In the face of all this, do words matter? A speech? A book? A shout of solidarity?

Are words poor weapons in the face of a phenomenon so ubiquitous and insidious?

My answer to that is a resounding no. Words can and do change the world.

An unseen, undefined enemy is infinitely more frightening than one dragged into the light.

Looking back on the decade since the misogyny speech, the biggest thing that stands out to me is the sea change in how we see and describe the world. Now, we don't accept it at face value. Instead we point to the lurking sexist and misogynistic forces at play.

This is what has been achieved through the #MeToo movement, the revival of women's history, the examination of gender biases in data, the sharing of the psychology of sexism and the identification of the gender barriers in work, politics, the law and civil society.

Now, if we see a woman politician being criticised by an opponent as cold and unlikeable, an answering voice will describe the sexist stereotype that is likely being used. Think of the reaction to then President Trump calling Kamala Harris 'nasty' when she was first announced as the vice-presidential candidate.

Now, if a photo of a powerful group of men is published, people will immediately ask, where are the women?

Now, a political party can pay an electoral price for ignoring women.

We see the world differently and we use our words to describe the manifest gender inequality.

This is a vital process, because the more we analyse, categorise and describe misogyny and its impacts, the easier it becomes to stand up to it now and ultimately defeat it.

I believe this so profoundly that it motivated me to establish the Global Institute for Women's Leadership at King's College London, and I am delighted we now have our sister Institute at the Australian National University. Research, facts and evidence can help us get to grips with the creeping cancer of misogyny and develop strategies for putting an end to it.

But, as meritorious as this work is, on its own it will never be enough. It will only catalyse change if what is learnt goes on to be applied in workplaces, parliaments, courts of law, newsrooms, community centres, homes and everywhere human beings gather.

That means it will only bring us a more gender equal future if campaigners in their millions carry the message.

Misogyny will end when we all come together to call it out and then demand immediate and effective action to eradicate it. A marrying of words, minds and decisive campaigning, all fuelled by impatient energy, because the world should already be better than it is.

If that seems daunting, then ask yourself this: Who would you be if, from your youngest moments, you had never spent your time and energy wondering whether you were being judged, patronised, excluded or threatened simply because of your gender? Who would you be if the very concept of gender inequality had never crossed your mind, because it was never a feature of your world? How would you feel?

I think it would feel like putting down a heavy load; relief mixed with a new-found sense of being lighter, freer and unencumbered.

I want that for every woman and every girl. In fact, I want for everyone on earth the sense of openness and inclusion that would come if gender inequality was something that only existed in history books.

And we can get there together.

Obviously, there will be carping critics and curmudgeons who will want to stand in our way. But we don't have to listen to any lectures from them. Not now, not ever.

Notes

2 In the media: Reporting on gender and the misogyny speech

1 Grattan, Michelle, 'Finessing a flagrant backflip', *Sydney Morning Herald*, 26 June 2010, smh.com.au/politics/federal/finessing-a-flagrant-backflip-20100625-z9t4.html, accessed 14 July 2022

2 Chan, Gabrielle, 'Julia Gillard explains "misogyny speech"', *The Guardian*, 30 September 2013, theguardian.com/world/2013/sep/30/julia-gillard-explains-misogyny-speech, accessed 14 June 2022

3 Hurst, Daniel, 'Obama White House team watched Julia Gillard's misogyny speech when annoyed at Tony Abbott', *The Guardian*, 30 April 2020, theguardian.com/australia-news/2020/apr/30/obama-white-house-watched-julia-gillards-misogyny-speech-when-annoyed-at-tony-abbott, accessed 14 June 2022

3 Choirs, TikToks and tea towels: How the misogyny speech travelled around the world

1 Harmon, Steph, 'Julia Gillard's misogyny speech voted "most unforgettable" moment in Australian TV history', *The Guardian*, 7 February 2020, theguardian.com/tv-and-radio/2020/feb/07/julia-gillard-misogyny-speech-voted-most-unforgettable-moment-in-australian-tv-history, accessed 8 June 2022

2 ABC News (Australia), 'Julia Gillard's "misogyny speech" in full (2012)', YouTube, 9 October 2012, youtu.be/ihd7ofrwQX0, accessed 8 June 2022

3 'Gillard's misogyny speech goes global', ABC News, 10 October 2012, abc.
   net.au/news/2012-10-10/international-reaction-to-gillard-speech/4305294,
   accessed 11 July 2022

4 Lester, Amelia, 'Ladylike: Julia Gillard's misogyny speech', *New Yorker*,
   9 October 2012, newyorker.com/online/blogs/newsdesk/2012/10/julia-gillards-
   misogyny-speech.html, accessed 8 June 2022

5 Morrissey, Tracie Egan, 'Best thing you'll see all day: Australia's female
   Prime Minister rips misogynist a new one in epic speech on sexism', Jezebel,
   9 October 2012, jezebel.com/best-thing-youll-see-all-day-australias-female-
   prime-m-5950163, accessed 8 June 2022

6 Summers, Anne, 'Gone is the turned cheek: Gillard as we've rarely seen her',
   ABC News, 10 October 2012, abc.net.au/news/2012-10-10/summers-gillard-
   sexism/4305728, accessed 11 July 2022; Whyte, Sally, 'Gillard fires up, Slipper
   fired: The pundits' verdict', Crikey, 10 October 2012, crikey.com.au/2012/10/10/
   gillard-fires-up-slipper-fired-the-pundits-verdict, accessed 11 July 2022

7 'Gillard bares all', *Sydney Morning Herald*, 24 January 2005, smh.com.au/
   national/gillard-bares-all-20050124-gdkjww.html, accessed 11 July 2022

8 Murphy, Katharine, 'Julia Gillard asked by radio station if her partner Tim
   Mathieson is gay', *The Guardian*, 13 June 2013, theguardian.com/world/2013/
   jun/13/julia-gillard-howard-sattler-interview, accessed 15 June 2022

9 Taylor, Lenore, 'PM's speech did stir hearts, but remember the context', *Sydney
   Morning Herald*, 13 October 2012, smh.com.au/politics/federal/pms-speech-
   did-stir-hearts-but-remember-the-context-20121012-27i1h.html,   accessed
   11 July 2020

10 Women in Journalism, 'Seen but not heard: How women make front page news',
   report, Women in Journalism, 15 October 2012, womeninjournal.wpengine.
   com/wp-content/uploads/2018/02/Seen_but_not_heard1.pdf, accessed 14 June
   2022

11 Probyn, Andrew, Georgia Hitch and Stephanie Dalzell, 'Finance Minister warns
   other Coalition staffers involved in lewd Parliament sex acts will be sacked',
   ABC News, 22 March 2021, abc.net.au/news/2021-03-22/coalition-staffer-
   lewd-sex-act-parliament-house-sacked/100022032, accessed 16 June 2022

12 Maiden, Samantha, 'Peta Credlin claims historical gay "orgies" took place
   at Parliament House', news.com.au, 25 March 2021, news.com.au/national/
   politics/peta-credlin-claims-historical-gay-orgies-took-place-at-parliament-
   house/news-story/e2615b83019bcfd71d15a6a8b73a26ec, accessed 16 June 2022

13 McMahon, Barbara, 'Sheilas put the mockers on ockers', *The Guardian*,
   11 November 2007, theguardian.com/world/2007/nov/11/australia.gender,
   accessed 2 August 2022

14 'Tony Abbott: Ex-Australian PM appointed UK trade adviser', BBC News, 4 September 2022, bbc.com/news/uk-politics-54027762, accessed 14 June 2022

15 Johnson, Boris, 'Welcome to Doughty Street', *The Spectator*, 17/24 December 2005, spectator.co.uk/article/17-24-december-2005-welcome-to-doughty-street, accessed 15 June 2022

16 Johnson, Boris, 'The male sex is to blame for the appalling proliferation of single mothers', *The Spectator*, 19 August 1995, archive.spectator.co.uk/article/19th-august-1995/6/politics, accessed 15 June 2022

17 minorfauna, 'After multiple requests, I bring you my take on the ICONIC "Misogyny" speech by Julia Gillard with a #glambot twist. #bosschallenge #quarantine', TikTok, 31 March 2020, tiktok.com/@minorfauna/video/6810199714819050758, accessed 8 June 2022; Videos: original sound by minorfauna, tiktok.com/music/original-sound-6810197035073964805, accessed 8 June 2022

18 Scabz – Topic, 'Julia Gillard's Misogyny Speech', YouTube, 26 November 2020, youtu.be/MSqtM89mBdg, accessed 8 June 2022

19 Bronwyn Calcutt, 'The Bad Thing – Julia's Misogyny Speech', YouTube, 9 November 2013, youtu.be/2Sr2aWd1MRs, accessed 8 June 2022

20 AustralianVoices, '"Not Now, Not Ever!" (Gillard Misogyny Speech)', YouTube, 16 March 2014, youtu.be/tpavaM62Fgo, accessed 8 June 2022

21 'After Julia', Decibel New Music Ensemble, decibelnewmusic.com/after-julia, accessed 8 June 2022

22 productionART theatre&events, 'MIGHTY "I Was Offended" (Julia Gillard Misogyny Speech Scene)', YouTube, 20 March 2019, youtu.be/6mhQgOcuMHo, accessed 8 June 2022

23 'Julia: The challenge of a woman in charge', Steamworks Arts, steamworks.net.au/projects/thatwomanjulia, accessed 8 June 2022

24 Israel, Janine, '"It keeps me alive": The politically potent bark paintings of Dhambit Munuŋgurr', *The Guardian*, 6 December 2021, theguardian.com/artanddesign/2021/dec/06/it-keeps-me-alive-the-politically-potent-bark-paintings-of-dhambit-munugurr, accessed 8 June 2022

25 Nally, Alicia, 'Women's March 4 Justice: Thousands march at rallies around Australia to protest against gendered violence', ABC News, 15 March 2022, abc.net.au/news/2021-03-15/live-blog-canberra-women-march-4-justice-sexual-assault/13246896, accessed 15 June 2022

4   The history and culture of misogyny, from the ancient world to today

1 Semonides, fragment 7, 74–7, 85–93, translation M. Beard

2 Euripides, *Hippolytus*, 616–41, translation J. Morwood, with adaptations

3   Homer, *Odyssey 1*, 356–9, translation M. Beard

4   Beard, Mary, *Women and Power*, Profile Books, London, 2017

5   Misogyny and intersectionality

1   Benard, Akeia A. F., 'Colonizing Black female bodies within patriarchal capital-ism: Feminist and human rights perspectives', *Sexualization, Media, & Society*, 2(4), 2016

2   Mothoagae, Itumeleng Daniel, 'Reclaiming our Black bodies: Reflections on a portrait of Sarah (Saartjie) Baartman and the destruction of Black bodies by the state', *Acta Theologica*, 2016(supp. 24), 2016, pp. 62–83

3   Brazilian Report, 'Slavery in Brazil', Think Brazil (blog), 13 May 2020, wilsoncenter.org/blog-post/slavery-brazil, accessed 29 April 2022

4   Crenshaw, Kimberlé, 'Mapping the margins: Intersectionality, identity politics, and violence against women of color', *Stanford Law Review*, 43(6), 1991, pp. 1241–99

5   Cambridge University Press, 'Misogyny', definition from *Cambridge Advanced Learner's Dictionary & Thesaurus*, dictionary.cambridge.org/dictionary/english/misogyny, accessed 29 April 2022

6   Clark, Treena, Shannan Dodson, Nancia Guivarra and Yatu Widders Hunt, '"We're not treated equally as Indigenous people or as women": The perspectives and experiences of Indigenous women in Australian public relations', *Public Relations Inquiry*, 10(2), 2021, pp. 163–83

7   Hamad, Ruby, *White Tears/Brown Scars*, Orion Publishing, London, 2020, p. 48

8   Spelman, Elizabeth V., *Inessential Woman: Problems of exclusion in feminist thought*, Beacon Press, Boston, 2002, p. ix

9   Lloyd, Moya, *Beyond Identity Politics: Feminism, power & politics*, SAGE Publications, London, 2005

10   Hamad, p. 27

11   Lowe, Lisa, 'Orient as woman, orientalism as sentimentalism: Flaubert', in *Critical Terrains: French and British orientalisms*, Cornell University Press, Ithaca, New York, 1991, pp. 75–101

12   Ryan, Tess, 'This Black body is not yours for the taking', in Bianca Fileborn and Rachel Loney-Howes (eds), *#MeToo and the Politics of Social Change*, Palgrave Macmillan, Cham, Switzerland, 2019, pp. 117–32

13   McQuire, Amy, 'Mainstream feminism still blind to its racism', IndigenousX, 6 March 2018, indigenousx.com.au/amy-mcquire-mainstream-feminism-still-blind-to-its-racism, accessed 29 April 2022

14   Mason-Bish, Hannah and Irene Zempi, 'Misogyny, racism, and Islamophobia: Street harassment at the intersections', *Feminist Criminology*, 14(5), 2019, pp. 540–59

15 'Serena Williams: Cartoonist denies US Open depiction is racist', BBC News, 11 September 2018, bbc.com/news/world-australia-45479954, accessed 29 April 2022

16 'Controversial Serena Williams cartoon did not breach media standards, Press Council finds', ABC News, 25 February 2019, abc.net.au/news/2019-02-25/serena-williams-cartoon-by-mark-knight-not-breach-of-standards/10844900, accessed 28 April 2022

17 Bailey, Moya, *Misogynoir Transformed: Black women's digital resistance*, New York University Press, New York, 2021

18 ibid.

19 Bailey, Moya and Trudy, 'On misogynoir: Citation, erasure, and plagiarism', *Feminist Media Studies*, 18(4), 2018, pp. 762–8

20 Fiuza, Camila, 'Four years without Marielle: A living legacy in politics for Black Brazilian women', RioOnWatch, 24 March 2022, rioonwatch.org/?p=69909, accessed 29 April 2022

21 ibid.

22 '#ruinablackgirlsmonday', Representations of Black Womanhood (blog), 16 May 2015, blackwomanhood.wordpress.com/2015/05/16/ruinablackgirl-monday, accessed 29 April 2022

23 Spelman, *Inessential Woman*

24 Daniels, Jessie, 'The trouble with white feminism: Whiteness, digital feminism and the intersectional internet', 16 February 2015, available at SSRN: ssrn.com/abstract=2569369, accessed 29 April 2022

25 ibid.

26 Lowe, 'Orient as woman, orientalism as sentimentalism: Flaubert'

27 McShane, Julianne, 'The world paid attention to Sarah Everard's killing. What about the women of color whose stories go untold?', The Lily, 25 March 2021, thelily.com/the-world-paid-attention-to-sarah-everards-killing-what-about-the-women-of-color-whose-stories-go-untold, accessed 29 April 2022

28 Bailey, Mary, 'How Black and Indigenous women are detrimentally affected by "missing white woman syndrome"', UAB Institute for Human Rights Blog, 1 November 2021, sites.uab.edu/humanrights/2021/11/01/how-black-and-indigenous-women-are-detrimentally-affected-by-missing-white-woman-syndrome, accessed 29 April 2022

29 United Nations Office on Drugs and Crime, 'Global Study on Homicide: Gender-related killing of women and girls 2019', report, UNODC, Vienna, Austria, 2019, unodc.org/documents/data-and-analysis/gsh/Booklet_5.pdf, accessed 17 May 2022

30 ibid.

31 Clark et al., "'We're not treated equally as Indigenous people or as women": The perspectives and experiences of Indigenous women in Australian public relations'

32 Buxton-Namisnyk, Emma, 'Domestic violence policing of First Nations women in Australia: "Settler" frameworks, consequential harms and the promise of meaningful self-determination', *British Journal of Criminology*, 2021, p. azab103

33 Morgan, Amanda and Karen Iles, 'The unique challenges faced by First Nations women in reporting workplace sexual harassment & assault', Fired Up, Refinery29, 22 September 2021, refinery29.com/en-au/workplace-sexual-harassment-first-nations, accessed 29 April 2022

34 Bailey, Jane and Sara Shayan, 'The missing and murdered Indigenous women crisis: Technological dimensions', in Jane Bailey, Asher Flynn and Nicola Henry (eds), *The Emerald International Handbook of Technology-Facilitated Violence and Abuse*, Emerald Publishing Limited, Bingley, United Kingdom, 2021

35 OCRCC, 'Position statement: Violence impacting Indigenous people and communities', Ontario Coalition of Rape Crisis Centres, 16 June 2021, sexualassaultsupport.ca/violence-impacting-indigenous-people-and-communities, accessed 29 April 2022

36 Mijatović, Dunja, 'No space for violence against women and girls in the digital world', Council of Europe: Commissioner for Human Rights, 15 March 2022, coe.int/en/web/commissioner/-/no-space-for-violence-against-women-and-girls-in-the-digital-world, accessed 29 April 2022

37 Hirji, Faiza, 'Claiming our space: Muslim women, activism, and social media', *Islamophobia Studies Journal*, 6(1), 2021, pp. 78–92

38 Czylwik, Ute, 'Digital violence against women: What needs to be done now', Heinrich-Böll-Stiftung (Heinrich Böll Foundation), 1 December 2021, eu.boell.org/en/2021/12/01/digital-violence-against-women-what-needs-be-done-now, accessed 17 May 2022

39 Mijatović, 'No space for violence against women and girls in the digital world'

40 Dhrodia, Azmina, 'Unsocial media: Tracking Twitter abuse against women MPs', Amnesty Global Insights, Medium, 4 September 2017, medium.com/@AmnestyInsights/unsocial-media-tracking-twitter-abuse-against-women-mps-fc28aeca498a, accessed 29 April 2022

41 ibid.

42 Bailey, *Misogynoir Transformed*

43 Daniels, 'The trouble with white feminism: Whiteness, digital feminism and the intersectional internet'

44 WPCC Editorial Board (University of Westminster), "'Intersectionality went viral": Toxic platforms, distinctive Black cyberfeminism and fighting

misogynoir – An interview with Kishonna Gray', *Westminster Papers in Communication and Culture*, 15(1), 2020, pp. 68–73

6 Sexism today: Tools in the patriarchy's toolbox

1 'Gillard's speech prompts misogyny definition rethink', ABC News, 17 October 2012, abc.net.au/news/2012-10-17/misogyny-redefined-after-gillard-speech/4317468, accessed 14 July 2022

2 Bates, Laura and contributors, The Everyday Sexism Project, everydaysexism. com, accessed 24 June 2022

3 Council of Europe, 'Sexism: See it, name it, stop it!', report, Council of Europe, September 2020, rm.coe.int/brochure-sexism/16809fba84, accessed 24 June 2022

4 APA Dictionary of Psychology, 'Sexism', American Psychological Association, dictionary.apa.org/sexism, accessed 26 June 2022

5 Brandt, Mark J., 'Sexism and gender inequality across 57 societies', *Psychological Science*, 22(11), 2011, pp. 1413–18

6 Zehnter, Miriam K. and Michelle K. Ryan, ongoing EU research project 'Contemporary sexism – nature, prevalence, consequences, and strategic use', supported through the European Union's Horizon 2020 research and innovation program. Further information and latest results can be found at miriam-zehnter.com/research/contemporary-sexism

7 UN DESA Statistics Division, 'Time spent in unpaid work; total work burden; and work-life balance', UN Department of Economic and Social Affairs, 8 March 2021, worlds-women-2020-data-undesa.hub.arcgis.com/apps/undesa::time-spent-in-unpaid-work-total-work-burden-and-work-life-balance/explore, accessed 28 July 2022

8 Swim, Janet K. and Laurie L. Cohen, 'Overt, covert, and subtle sexism. A comparison between the Attitudes Towards Women and Modern Sexism Scales', *Psychology of Women Quarterly*, 21(1), 1997, pp. 103–18

9 Zehnter and Ryan, ongoing EU research project 'Contemporary sexism – nature, prevalence, consequences, and strategic use'

10 Herrero, Juan, Francisco J. Rodríguez and Andrea Torres, 'Acceptability of partner violence in 51 societies: The role of sexism and attitudes toward violence in social relationships', *Violence Against Women*, 23(3), 2017, pp. 351–67

11 Suarez, Eliana and Tahany M. Gadalla, 'Stop blaming the victim: A meta-analysis on rape myths', *Journal of Interpersonal Violence*, 25(11), 2010, pp. 2010–35

12 Glick, Peter and Susan T. Fiske, 'The ambivalent sexism inventory: Differentiating hostile and benevolent sexism', *Journal of Personality and Social Psychology*, 70(3), 1996, pp. 491–512

13 Zehnter and Ryan, ongoing EU research project 'Contemporary sexism – nature, prevalence, consequences, and strategic use'

14 Swim, Janet K., Lauri L. Hyers, Laurie L. Cohen and Melissa J. Ferguson, 'Everyday sexism: Evidence for its incidence, nature, and psychological impact from three daily diary studies', *Journal of Social Issues*, 57(1), 2001, 31–53

15 Ramos, Miguel, Manuela Barreto, Naomi Ellemers, Miguel Moya and Lúcia Ferreira, 'What hostile and benevolent sexism communicate about men's and women's warmth and competence', *Group Processes & Intergroup Relations*, 21(1), 2018, pp. 159–77

16 Russell, Brenda L. and Kristin Y. Trigg, 'Tolerance of sexual harassment: An examination of gender differences, ambivalent sexism, social dominance, and gender roles', *Sex Roles*, 50(7–8), 2004, pp. 565–73

17 Saunders, Benjamin A., Crista Scaturro, Christopher Guarino and Elspeth Kelly, 'Contending with catcalling: The role of system-justifying beliefs and ambivalent sexism in predicting women's coping experiences with (and men's attributions for) stranger harassment', *Current Psychology*, 36(2), 2017, 324–38

18 Cross, Emily J., Nickola C. Overall, Matthew D. Hammond and Garth J. O. Fletcher, 'When does men's hostile sexism predict relationship aggression? The moderating role of partner commitment', *Social Psychological and Personality Science*, 8(3), 2017, pp. 331–40

19 Martinez-Pecino, Roberto and Mercedes Durán, 'I love you but I cyberbully you: The role of hostile sexism', *Journal of Interpersonal Violence*, 34(4), 2019, pp. 812–25

20 Abrams, Dominic, G., Tendayi Viki, Barbara Masser and Gerd Bohner, 'Perceptions of stranger and acquaintance rape: The role of benevolent and hostile sexism in victim blame and rape proclivity', *Journal of Personality and Social Psychology*, 84(1), 2003, pp. 111–25

21 Zehnter and Ryan, ongoing EU research project 'Contemporary sexism – nature, prevalence, consequences, and strategic use'

22 Bradley-Geist, Jill C., Ivy Rivera and Susan D. Geringer, 'The collateral damage of ambient sexism: Observing sexism impacts bystander self-esteem and career aspirations', *Sex Roles*, 73(1–2), 2015, pp. 29–42

23 Swim and Cohen, 'Overt, covert, and subtle sexism. A comparison between the Attitudes Towards Women and Modern Sexism Scales'

24 Zehnter and Ryan, ongoing EU research project 'Contemporary sexism – nature, prevalence, consequences, and strategic use'

25 ibid.

26 Grosch, Kerstin, Katharina Gangl, Florian Spitzer and Anna Walter, 'Women in leadership positions in tech professions', unpublished report commissioned by Federal Ministry for Digital and Economic Affairs (Austria), 2019

27 Keogh, Louise A., Lyle C. Gurrin and Patricia Moore, 'Estimating the abortion rate in Australia from National Hospital Morbidity and Pharmaceutical Benefits Scheme data', *Medical Journal of Australia*, 215(8), 2021, pp. 375–6

28 Jones, Rachel K. and Jenna Jerman, 'Population group abortion rates and lifetime incidence of abortion: United States, 2008–2014', *American Journal of Public Health*, 107(12), 2017, pp. 1904–9

29 Glick, Peter and Susan T. Fiske, 'An ambivalent alliance: Hostile and benevolent sexism as complementary justifications for gender inequality', *American Psychologist*, 56(2), 2001, 109–18

30 Eagly, Alice H. and Antonio Mladinic, 'Are people prejudiced against women? Some answers from research on attitudes, gender stereotypes, and judgments of competence', *European Review of Social Psychology*, 5, 1994, pp. 1–35

31 Brown-Iannuzzi, Jazmin L., Erin Cooley, William Cipolli and Sarita Mehta, 'Race, ambivalent sexism, and perceptions of situations when police shoot Black women', *Social Psychological and Personality Science*, 13(1), 2022, pp. 127–38

32 Ramos et al., 'What hostile and benevolent sexism communicate about men's and women's warmth and competence'

33 'Julie Bishop: The loyal girl', *West Australian*, 1 December 2009, thewest.com.au/news/wa/julie-bishop-the-loyal-girl-ng-ya-228850, accessed 14 July 2022

34 Huang, Yanshu, Paul G. Davies, Chris G. Sibley and Danny Osborne, 'Benevolent sexism, attitudes toward motherhood, and reproductive rights', *Personality and Social Psychology Bulletin*, 42(7), 2016, pp. 970–84

35 Young, Lauren M. and Margaret M. Nauta, 'Sexism as a predictor of attitudes toward women in the military and in combat', *Military Psychology*, 25(2), 2013, pp. 166–71

36 Goh, Jin X. and Judith A. Hall, 'Nonverbal and verbal expressions of men's sexism in mixed-gender interactions', *Sex Roles*, 72(5–6), 2015, pp. 252–61

37 King, Eden B., Whitney Botsford, Michelle R. Hebl, Stephanie Kazama, Jeremy F. Dawson and Andrew Perkins, 'Benevolent sexism at work: Gender differences in the distribution of challenging developmental experiences', *Journal of Management*, 2012, 38(6), pp. 1835–66

38 Swim, Janet K., Robyn Mallett, Yvonne Russo-Devosa and Charles Stangor, 'Judgments of sexism: A comparison of the subtlety of sexism measures and sources of variability in judgments of sexism', *Psychology of Women Quarterly*, 29(4), 2005, pp. 406–11

39 Dardenne, Benoit, Muriel Dumont and Thierry Bollier, 'Insidious dangers of benevolent sexism: Consequences for women's performance', *Journal of Personality and Social Psychology*, 93(5), 2007, pp. 764–79

40 Hammond, Matthew D. and Nickola C. Overall, 'Benevolent sexism and support of romantic partner's goals: Undermining women's competence while fulfilling men's intimacy needs', *Personality and Social Psychology Bulletin*, 41(9), 2015, pp. 1180–94

41 Roberts, Steven O., Arnold K. Ho, Marjorie Rhodes and Susan A. Gelman, 'Making boundaries great again: Essentialism and support for boundary-enhancing initiatives', *Personality and Social Psychology Bulletin*, 43(12), 2017, pp. 1643–58

42 Romano, Aja, 'Google has fired the engineer whose anti-diversity memo reflects a divided tech culture', Vox, 8 August 2017, vox.com/identities/2017/8/8/16106728/google-fired-engineer-anti-diversity-memo, accessed 14 July 2022

43 Zehnter and Ryan, ongoing EU research project 'Contemporary sexism – nature, prevalence, consequences, and strategic use'

44 Fine, Cordelia, *Delusions of Gender: How our minds, society, and neurosexism create difference*, W. W. Norton & Company, New York, 2011

45 Carpenter, Christopher J., 'Meta-analyses of sex differences in responses to sexual versus emotional infidelity: Men and women are more similar than different', *Psychology of Women Quarterly*, 36(1), 2012, pp. 25–37

46 Eagly, Alice H. and Wendy Wood, 'The origins of sex differences in human behavior: Evolved dispositions versus social roles', *American Psychologist*, 54(6), 1999, pp. 408–23

47 Hyde, Janet Shibley, Rebecca S. Bigler, Daphna Joel, Charlotte Chucky Tate and Sari M. van Anders, 'The future of sex and gender in psychology: Five challenges to the gender binary', *American Psychologist*, 74(2), 2019, pp. 171–93

48 Fine, Cordelia, *Testosterone Rex: Myths of sex, science, and society*, W. W. Norton & Company, New York, 2017

49 Hyde et al., 'The future of sex and gender in psychology: Five challenges to the gender binary'

50 Swim, Janet K., Kathryn J. Aikin, Wayne S. Hall and Barbara A. Hunter, 'Sexism and racism: Old-fashioned and modern prejudices', *Journal of Personality and Social Psychology*, 68(2), 1995, pp. 199–214

51 Piscopo, Jennifer M. and Meryl Kenny, 'Rethinking the ambition gap: Gender and candidate emergence in comparative perspective', *European Journal of Politics and Gender*, 3(1), 2020, pp. 3–10

52 Zehnter and Ryan, ongoing EU research project 'Contemporary sexism – nature, prevalence, consequences, and strategic use'

53 Begeny, Christopher T., Michelle K. Ryan, Corinne A. Moss-Racusin and Gudrun Ravetz, 'In some professions, women have become well represented,

yet gender bias persists – perpetuated by those who think it is not happening', *Science Advances*, 6(26), 2020, p. eaba7814

54 Biggs, Jacklyn, Patricia H. Hawley and Monica Biernat, 'The academic conference as a chilly climate for women: Effects of gender representation on experiences of sexism, coping responses, and career intentions', *Sex Roles*, 78(5–6), 2018, pp. 394–408

55 Zehnter, Miriam K. and Christa Nater, 'Beyond being beneficiaries: Explaining why women have more favorable attitudes towards women quotas than men' (in review)

56 Ellemers, Naomi and Manuela Barreto, 'Collective action in modern times: How modern expressions of prejudice prevent collective action', *Journal of Social Issues*, 65(4), 2009, pp. 749–68

57 Zehnter, Miriam K., Francesca Manzi, Patrick E. Shrout and Madeline E. Heilman, 'Belief in sexism shift: Defining a new form of contemporary sexism and introducing the belief in sexism shift scale (BSS scale)', *PloS one*, 16(3), 2021, p. e0248374

58 Kehn, Andre and Joelle C. Ruthig, 'Perceptions of gender discrimination across six decades: The moderating roles of gender and age', *Sex Roles*, 69(5–6), 2013, pp. 289–96

59 Dutta, Nirmalya, 'Don't mancriminate – A sad marketing ploy to grab eyeballs', Feminism in India, 27 June 2015, feminisminindia.com/2015/06/27/dont-mancriminate-sad-marketing-ploy-grab-eyeballs, accessed 14 July 2022

60 World Economic Forum, 'Global Gender Gap Report 2021', report, World Economic Forum, 30 March 2021, weforum.org/reports/global-gender-gap-report-2021, accessed 14 July 2022

61 Zehnter et al., 'Belief in sexism shift: Defining a new form of contemporary sexism and introducing the belief in sexism shift scale (BSS scale)'

62 Zehnter, Miriam K., Francesca Manzi and Benjamin Ruisch, 'Gaining traction, belief in sexism shift increases and helps extremist leaders to power' (in preparation)

63 American National Election Studies, '2016 Time Series Study', ANES, electionstudies.org/data-center/2016-time-series-study, accessed 14 July 2022

64 Gallup, Inc. and the International Labour Organization, 'Regional tables and country/territory dashboards', report, ILO, 8 March 2017, ilo.org/wcmsp5/groups/public/---dgreports/---dcomm/documents/publication/wcms_546318.pdf, accessed 14 July 2022

65 Horowitz, Juliana Menasce, Kim Parker and Renee Stepler, 'Wide partisan gaps in US over how far the country has come on gender equality', Pew Research Center, 18 October 2017, pewresearch.org/social-trends/2017/10/18/

wide-partisan-gaps-in-u-s-over-how-far-the-country-has-come-on-gender-equality, accessed 14 July 2022

66 Zehnter and Ryan, ongoing EU research project 'Contemporary sexism – nature, prevalence, consequences, and strategic use'

67 Zehnter et al., 'Belief in sexism shift: Defining a new form of contemporary sexism and introducing the belief in sexism shift scale (BSS scale)'

68 Harsey, Sarah and Jennifer J. Freyd, 'Deny, attack, and reverse victim and offender (DARVO): What is the influence on perceived perpetrator and victim credibility?', *Journal of Aggression, Maltreatment & Trauma*, 29(8), pp. 897–916

7 Misogyny and violence

1 Atwood, Margaret, *Second Words: Selected critical prose*, Anansi, Toronto, 1982, p. 413

2 Hill, Jess, *See What You Made Me Do: Power, control and domestic violence*, Black Inc., Carlton, 2019

3 Meagher, Tom, 'The danger of the monster myth', ABC News, 18 April 2014, abc.net.au/news/2014-04-18/meagher-the-danger-of-the-monster-myth/5399108, accessed 14 July 2022

4 Ireland, Judith, 'Malcolm Turnbull's scathing attack on men who commit domestic violence', *Sydney Morning Herald*, 24 September 2015, smh.com.au/politics/federal/malcolm-turnbulls-scathing-attack-on-men-who-commit-domestic-violence-20150924-gjtpqt.html, accessed 14 July 2022

5 Gelles, Richard J. and Murray A. Straus, 'Violence in the American family', *Journal of Social Issues*, 35(2), 1979, pp. 15–39

6 Hill, Jess, 'What I've learned about domestic violence in my year reporting on it', *The Guardian*, 11 September 2015, theguardian.com/commentisfree/2015/sep/11/most-people-dont-get-domestic-violence-because-it-doesnt-make-sense, accessed 14 July 2022

7 Summers, Anne, 'The Choice: Violence or poverty', report, University of Technology Sydney, 2022, violenceorpoverty.com, accessed 19 July 2022

8 Boxall, Hayley and Anthony Morgan, 'Experiences of coercive control among Australian women', AIC Statistical Bulletin 30, Australian Institute of Criminology, Canberra, 2021, apo.org.au/node/311353, accessed 19 July 2022

9 'Understanding family violence and the risks of insurance', report, Allianz, November 2021, allianz.com.au/images/internet/allianz-au/Understanding%20Family%20Violence%20and%20the%20risks%20of%20Insurance.pdf, accessed 14 July 2022

10 Greer, Germaine, *On Rage*, Melbourne University Press, Carlton, Victoria, 2018

11 Fromm, Erich, *The Anatomy of Human Destructiveness*, Penguin, Harmondsworth, 1973, p. 323

12 Hill, Jess, 'Episode 3: Why do they do it?', *The Trap*, podcast (transcript), Victorian Women's Trust, vwt.org.au/the-trap-ep03-transcript, accessed 14 July 2022

13 Blair, Elizabeth, 'Women are speaking up about harassment and abuse, but why now?', NPR, 27 October 2017, npr.org/2017/10/27/560231232/women-are-speaking-up-about-harassment-and-abuse-but-why-now, accessed 14 July 2022

14 Hill, 'Episode 3: Why do they do it?'

8   Misogyny in politics: 'There's just something about her'

1 Goodman, Lawrence, 'How the Access Hollywood tape affected the 2016 election', Brandeis NOW, 30 September 2020, brandeis.edu/now/2020/september/access-hollywood-greenlee.html, accessed 26 June 2022

2 Cummings, William and Eliza Collins, 'Here are 12 women who made allegations against Trump this week', USA Today, 13 October 2016, usatoday.com/story/news/politics/onpolitics/2016/10/13/roundup-accusations-bad-behavior-hit-trump-wednesday/91984974, accessed 26 June 2022

3 Zhou, Li, 'A historic new Congress will be sworn in today', Vox, 3 January 2019, vox.com/2018/12/6/18119733/congress-diversity-women-election-good-news, accessed 26 June 2022

4 Blazina, Carrie and Drew Desilver, 'A record number of women are serving in the 117th Congress', Pew Research Center, 15 January 2021, pewresearch.org/fact-tank/2021/01/15/a-record-number-of-women-are-serving-in-the-117th-congress, accessed 26 June 2022

5 Center for American Women and Politics, 'Women in elective office 2022', CAWP, Eagleton Institute of Politics, Rutgers University–New Brunswick, 2022, cawp.rutgers.edu/facts/current-numbers/women-elective-office-2022, accessed 26 June 2022

6 Sullivan, Sean and Annie Linskey, 'The explosive question for Democrats: Can a woman defeat Trump in November?', *Washington Post*, 14 January 2020, washingtonpost.com/politics/the-explosive-question-for-democrats-can-a-woman-defeat-trump-in-november/2020/01/14/502b4110-36d9-11ea-bb7b-265f4554af6d_story.html, accessed 26 June 2022

7 Nash, Elizabeth, Lauren Cross and Joerg Dreweke, '2022 state legislative sessions: Abortion bans and restrictions on medication abortion dominate', Guttmacher Institute, 16 March 2022 guttmacher.org/article/2022/03/2022-state-legislative-sessions-abortion-bans-and-restrictions-medication-abortion, accessed 26 June 2022

8 Dann, Carrie, 'Hillary Clinton's popularity has fluctuated during decades in public eye', NBC News, 13 April 2015, nbcnews.com/meet-the-press/numbers-when-america-loved-hated-hillary-n338836, accessed 26 June 2022

9 Barbara Lee Family Foundation, 'Shared hurdles: How political races change when two women compete', report, BLFF, 2022, barbaraleefoundation.org/wp-content/uploads/4.25-FINAL-2022-Woman-v.-Woman-memo.pdf, accessed 26 June 2022

10 Sarlin, Benjy, 'Why "Medicare for All" wrecked Elizabeth Warren but not Bernie Sanders', NBC News, 6 March 2020, nbcnews.com/politics/2020-election/why-medicare-all-wrecked-elizabeth-warren-not-bernie-sanders-n1150691, accessed 26 June 2022

11 Blachor, Devorah, 'I don't hate women candidates – I just hated Hillary and coincidentally I'm starting to hate Elizabeth Warren', McSweeney's Internet Tendency, 2 January 2019, mcsweeneys.net/articles/i-dont-hate-women-candidates-i-just-hated-hillary-and-coincidentally-im-starting-to-hate-elizabeth-warren, accessed 26 June 2022

12 '"I have a plan for that." Elizabeth Warren is betting that Americans are ready for her big ideas', *TIME*, 9 May 2019, time.com/magazine/us/5586396/may-20th-2019-vol-193-no-19-u-s, accessed 26 June 2022

9   Misogyny in today's world of work

1 hooks, bell, *Feminist Theory: From margin to center*, Harvard University Press, Cambridge, Massachusetts, 1984

2 Code, Lorraine (ed.), *Encyclopedia of Feminist Theories*, Routledge, London, 2002

3 Acker, Joan, 'Hierarchies, jobs, bodies: A theory of gendered organizations', *Gender & Society*, 4(2), 1990, pp. 139–58

4 Hinchliffe, Emma, 'The female CEOs on this year's Fortune 500 just broke three all-time records', *Fortune*, 2 June 2021, fortune.com/2021/06/02/female-ceos-fortune-500-2021-women-ceo-list-roz-brewer-walgreens-karen-lynch-cvs-thasunda-brown-duckett-tiaa, accessed 13 June 2022

5 International Labour Organization, 'Global wage report 2020–21: Wages and minimum wages in the time of COVID-19', report, ILO, Geneva, 2020, ilo.org/wcmsp5/groups/public/---dgreports/---dcomm/---publ/documents/publication/wcms_762534.pdf, accessed 16 May 2022

6 Duffy, Mignon and Amy Armenia, 'Paid care work around the globe: A comparative analysis of 47 countries and territories', discussion paper 39, UN Women, New York, April 2021

7   Charlton, Emma, '7 out of 10 global health leaders are men: Study', World Economic Forum, 16 April 2020, weforum.org/agenda/2020/04/global-health-leadership-gender-equality-report, accessed 17 May 2022

8   Global Institute for Women's Leadership, King's College London and Ipsos, 'International Women's Day 2022', report, GIWL, London, March 2022 kcl.ac.uk/giwl/assets/iwd-survey-2022.pdf, accessed 17 May 2022

9   Kalev, Alexandra and Gal Deutsch, 'Gender inequality and workplace organizations: Understanding reproduction and change', in *Handbook of the Sociology of Gender*, Barbara J. Risman, Carissa M. Froyum and William J. Scarborough (eds), Springer International Publishing, Cham, Switzerland, 2018, pp. 257–69

10 Saccomano, Celeste, 'Sexual harassment in the informal economy: Farmworkers and domestic workers', report, UN Women, New York, 2020, unwomen.org/sites/default/files/Headquarters/Attachments/Sections/Library/Publications/2020/Discussion-paper-Sexual-harassment-in-the-informal-economy-en.pdf, accessed 17 May 2022, p. 4

11 ibid.

12 ibid.

13 International Labour Organization, 'Care work and care jobs: For the future of decent work', report, ILO, Geneva, 2018, ilo.org/wcmsp5/groups/public/---dgreports/---dcomm/---publ/documents/publication/wcms_633135.pdf, accessed 16 May 2022

14 Haidar, Diala, 'A tribute to "Mary" on International Workers' Day', Amnesty International, 1 May 2022, amnesty.org/en/latest/news/2022/05/a-tribute-to-mary-on-workers-day, accessed 17 May 2022

15 International Labour Organization, 'Who are domestic workers', ILO, ilo.org/global/topics/domestic-workers/who/lang--en/index.htm, accessed 25 May 2022

16 Berdahl, Jennifer L., 'Harassment based on sex: Protecting social status in the context of gender hierarchy', *Academy of Management Review*, 32(2), 2007, p. 644

17 Saccomano, 'Sexual harassment in the informal economy: Farmworkers and domestic workers'

18 Connell, Raewyn, *Gender and Power: Society, the person and sexual politics*, Stanford University Press, Stanford, 1987

19 Cortina, Lilia M. and Maira A. Areguin, 'Putting people down and pushing them out: Sexual harassment in the workplace', *Annual Review of Organizational Psychology and Organizational Behavior*, 8(1), 2021, p. 287

20 Fitzgerald, Louise F., Michele J. Gelfand and Fritz Drasgow, 'Measuring sexual harassment: Theoretical and psychometric advances', *Basic and Applied Social Psychology*, 17(4), 1995, pp. 425–45

21 Johnson, Paula A., Sheila E. Widnall and Frazier F. Benya (eds), *Sexual Harassment of Women: Climate, culture, and consequences in academic sciences, engineering, and medicine*, National Academies Press, Washington, DC, 2018

22 Cortina and Areguin, 'Putting people down and pushing them out: Sexual harassment in the workplace'

23 Deloitte, 'Women @ Work 2022: A global outlook', report, Deloitte Touche Tohmatsu Limited, London, 2022, deloitte.com/content/dam/Deloitte/global/Documents/deloitte-women-at-work-2022-a-global-outlook.pdf, accessed 17 May 2022

24 Global Institute for Women's Leadership et al., 'International Women's Day 2022'

25 Smartt, Nicole, 'Sexual harassment in the workplace in a #MeToo world', *Forbes*, 20 December 2017, forbes.com/sites/forbeshumanresourcescouncil/2017/12/20/sexual-harassment-in-the-workplace-in-a-metoo-world, accessed 17 May 2022

26 Time Staff, '700,000 female farmworkers say they stand with Hollywood actors against sexual assault', *Time*, 10 November 2017, time.com/5018813/farmworkers-solidarity-hollywood-sexual-assault, accessed 17 May 2022

27 Pender, Kieran, 'Us too? Bullying and sexual harassment in the legal profession', report, International Bar Association, London, 2019, ibanet.org/MediaHandler?id=B29F6FEA-889F-49CF-8217-F8F7D78C2479, accessed 17 May 2022

28 Parker, Kim, 'Women in majority-male workplaces report higher rates of gender discrimination', Pew Research Center, 7 March 2018, pewresearch.org/fact-tank/2018/03/07/women-in-majority-male-workplaces-report-higher-rates-of-gender-discrimination, accessed 7 July 2022

29 60 Minutes Australia, 'EXPOSED: The Australian mining industry's darkest secret', YouTube, 20 March 2022, youtu.be/8CX3nJcTmhk, accessed 17 May 2022

30 Women Who Tech, 'The state of women in tech and startups: Top findings for 2020', Women Who Tech, 2020, womenwhotech.org/data-and-resources/state-women-tech-and-startups, accessed 17 May 2020

31 Edelman, Lauren B., *Working Law: Courts, corporations, and symbolic civil rights*, Chicago University Press, Chicago, 2016

32 Johnson et al. (eds), *Sexual Harassment of Women: Climate, culture, and consequences in academic sciences, engineering, and medicine*

33 Roehling, Mark V. and Jason Huang, 'Sexual harassment training effectiveness: An interdisciplinary review and call for research', *Journal of Organizational Behavior*, 39(2), 2018, pp. 134–50

34 Kwarteng, Kwasi, '"Some bad apples": Senior Tory minister denies institutional misogyny', *The Guardian*, 2 May 2022, theguardian.com/politics/2022/may/01/some-bad-apples-senior-tory-minister-denies-denies-institutional-misogyny, accessed 16 May 2022

35 Woods, Freya A. and Janet B. Ruscher, '"Calling-out" vs. "calling-in" prejudice: Confrontation style affects inferred motive and expected outcomes', *British Journal of Social Psychology*, 60(1), 2021, pp. 50–73

36 Cortina and Areguin, 'Putting people down and pushing them out: Sexual harassment in the workplace'

37 Dobbin, Frank and Alexandra Kalev, 'Are diversity programs merely ceremonial? Evidence-free institutionalization', in Royston Greenwood, Christine Oliver, Thomas B. Lawrence and Renate E. Meyer (eds), *The SAGE Handbook of Organizational Institutionalism*, SAGE Publications, London, 2017, pp. 808–28

38 Berdahl, Jennifer L., Marianne Cooper, Peter Glick, Robert W. Livingston and Joan C. Williams, 'Work as a masculinity contest', *Journal of Social Issues*, 74(3), 2018, pp. 422–48

39 Matos, Kenneth, Olivia O'Neill and Xue Lei, 'Toxic leadership and the masculinity contest culture: How "win or die" cultures breed abusive leadership', *Journal of Social Issues*, 74(3), 2018, pp. 500–28

40 Global Institute of Women's Leadership, King's College London, Working Families and University of East Anglia, 'Working parents, flexibility and job quality: What are the trade-offs?', report, Working Families and Family-friendly Working Scotland, 2018, kcl.ac.uk/giwl/assets/working-parents-flexibility-and-job-quality-what-are-the-trade-offs.pdf, accessed 16 May 2022

41 Charmes, Jacques, 'The unpaid care work and the labour market. An analysis of time use data based on the latest World Compilation of Time-use Surveys', report, International Labour Organization, 2019, ilo.org/wcmsp5/groups/public/---dgreports/---gender/documents/publication/wcms_732791.pdf, accessed 14 July 2022

42 Galea, Natalie, Abigail Powell, Martin Loosemore and Louise Chappell, 'Designing robust and revisable policies for gender equality: Lessons from the Australian construction industry', *Construction Management and Economics*, 33(5–6), 2015, pp. 375–89; Kelly, Erin L. and Phyllis Moen, *Overload: How good jobs went bad and what we can do about it*, Princeton University Press, Princeton, New Jersey, 2020

43 Chamorro-Premuzic, Tomas, *Why Do So Many Incompetent Men Become Leaders? (And how to fix it)*, Harvard Business Review Press, Boston, 2019

44 Gaucher, Danielle, Justin Friesen and Aaron C. Kay, 'Evidence that gendered wording in job advertisements exists and sustains gender inequality', *Journal of Personality and Psychology*, 101(1), 2011, pp. 109–28

45 LinkedIn, 'Language matters: How words impact men and women in the workplace', report, Global Institute for Women's Leadership, kcl.ac.uk/giwl/assets/linkedin-language-matters-report-final.pdf, accessed 16 May 2022

46 Gaston, Kevin C. and Jackie A. Alexander, 'Women in the police: Factors influencing managerial advancement', *Women in Management Review*, 12(2), 1997, pp. 47–55

47 Peters, Kim, Michelle K. Ryan and S. Alexander Haslam, 'Women's occupational motivation: The impact of being a woman in a man's world', in *Handbook of Research on Promoting Women's Careers*, Susan Vinnicombe, Ronald J. Burke, Stacy Blake-Beard and Lynda L. Moore (eds), Edward Elgar Publishing, Cheltenham, 2013, pp. 162–77

48 Joshi, Aparna, Jooyeon Son and Hyuntak Roh, 'When can women close the gap? A meta-analytic test of sex differences in performance and rewards', *Academy of Management Journal*, 58(5), 2015, pp. 1516–45

49 Leibbrandt, Andreas and John A. List, 'Do women avoid salary negotiations? Evidence from a large-scale natural field experiment', *Management Science*, 61(9), 2015, pp. 2016–24

50 Jones, Laura, 'Women's progression in the workplace', report, Government Equalities Office, London, 2019, assets.publishing.service.gov.uk/government/uploads/system/uploads/attachment_data/file/840404/KCL_Main_Report.pdf, accessed 17 May 2022, p. 4

51 Forscher, Patrick S., Calvin K. Lai, Jordan R. Axt, Charles R. Ebersole, Michelle Herman, Patricia G. Devine and Brian A. Nosek, 'A meta-analysis of procedures to change implicit measures', *Journal of Personality and Social Psychology*, 117(3), 2019, pp. 522–59

52 Payne, B. Keith, Alan J. Lambert and Larry L. Jacoby, 'Best laid plans: Effects of goals on accessibility bias and cognitive control in race-based misperceptions of weapons', *Journal of Experimental Social Psychology*, 38(4), 2002, pp. 384–96

53 Goldin, Claudia and Cecilia Rouse, 'Orchestrating impartiality: The impact of "blind" auditions on female musicians', *American Economic Review*, 90(4), 2000, pp. 715–41

54 Weck-Hannemann, Hannelore, 'Orchestrating impartiality: The impact of "blind" auditions on female musicians, by Claudia Goldin and Cecilia Rouse', in Bruno S. Frey and Christoph A. Schaltegger (eds) *21st Century Economics*, Springer, Cham, 2019, link.springer.com/chapter/10.1007/978-3-030-17740-9_57, accessed 14 July 2022

55 Goldin and Rouse, 'Orchestrating impartiality: The impact of "blind" auditions on female musicians'

56 Business in the Community, Santander and Global Institute for Women's Leadership, King's College London, 'Ensuring inclusive working cultures – What really works?', report, Business in the Community, London, 2021, kcl.ac.uk/giwl/assets/everyday-inclusion.pdf, accessed 16 May 2022

57 Duguid, Fiona and Nadya Weber, 'Women informal workers and the empowering nature of collectivizing and collectives: An evidence synthesis', report (draft), International Labour Organization, 7 July 2019, ilo.org/wcmsp5/groups/public/---ed_emp/---emp_ent/---coop/documents/genericdocument/wcms_743758.pdf, accessed 17 May 2022

58 International Labour Organization, 'Making decent work a reality for domestic workers: Progress and prospects in Asia and the Pacific ten years after the adoption of the Domestic Workers Convention, 2011 (No. 189)', report, ILO, 2021, ilo.org/wcmsp5/groups/public/---asia/---ro-bangkok/documents/publication/wcms_800224.pdf, accessed 17 May 2022

59 Cowper-Coles, Minna, Miriam Glennie, Aleida Mendes Borges and Caitlin Schmid., 'Bridging the gap? An analysis of gender pay gap reporting in six countries', King's College London, October 2021, kcl.ac.uk/giwl/research/bridging-the-gap, accessed 11 July 2022

10 What do next-generation activists think? In conversation with Chanel Contos, Caitlin Figueiredo and Sally Scales

1 Armstrong, Martin, 'It will take another 136 years to close the global gender gap', World Economic Forum, 12 April 2021, weforum.org/agenda/2021/04/136-years-is-the-estimated-journey-time-to-gender-equality, accessed 10 June 2022

2 'Uluru Statement from the Heart', ulurustatement.org, accessed 10 June 2022

Acknowledgements

My thanks go to all those who have contributed their wisdom and words to *Not Now, Not Ever*. I am keenly aware that when I first reached out it would have been easy to say, 'I'm already too stretched, too busy,' which would have been completely accurate. Instead, in a spirit of generosity, you cleared your desks, schedules and minds, and started to write. For that, I will be forever grateful.

To the Global Institute for Women's Leadership teams at King's College London and the Australian National University in Canberra, thanks for all the incredible work you do and for your many efforts towards this book. A special shout-out to Nora Jain and Dahae Suh for all your support.

To Meredith Curnow, Kathryn Knight, Karen Reid and all of the wonderful team at Penguin Random House Australia, as always you have been a delight to work with. Thanks for sticking with me through my various writing adventures.

I am also sincerely grateful for Penguin Random House's financial support of GIWL. Thank you for agreeing to donate a proportion of the usual publisher's earnings on book sales. Together with the donation of author's royalties from the sale of this book, that means every book bought is strengthening our research work.

And last, but by no means least, I want to express my heartfelt gratitude to the women in my office: Michelle, Connie, Roanna, Maeve and Nina. I know how hard you work, and I understand the trepidation you must feel every time I say, 'I've been thinking, and I've got an idea for a new project.' Thanks for always taking some deep breaths before you react, and for your unfailing enthusiasm.

An inspirational and practical book sharing the experience and advice of some of our most extraordinary women leaders, in their own words.

With broad experience on the world stage in politics, economics and global not-for-profits, Ngozi Okonjo-Iweala and Julia Gillard have some strong ideas about the impact of gender on the treatment of leaders. *Women and Leadership* takes a consistent and comprehensive approach to teasing out what is different for women who lead.

The authors present a lively and readable analysis of the influence of gender on women's access to positions of leadership, the perceptions of them as leaders, the trajectory of their leadership and the circumstances in which it comes to an end. By presenting the lessons that can be learned from women leaders, Julia and Ngozi provide a road map of essential knowledge to inspire us all, and an action agenda for change that allows women to take control and combat gender bias.

Featuring Jacinda Ardern, Hillary Clinton, Ellen Johnson Sirleaf, Theresa May, Michelle Bachelet, Joyce Banda, Erna Solberg and Christine Lagarde.

Discover a
new favourite